Fodor's
25 Best

EDINBURGH

How to Use This Book

KEY TO SYMBOLS	
✚ Map reference to the accompanying fold-out map	🚢 Nearest riverboat or ferry stop
✉ Address	♿ Facilities for visitors with disabilities
☎ Telephone number	❓ Other practical information
⏰ Opening/closing times	▷ Further information
🍽 Restaurant or café	ℹ Tourist information
🚆 Nearest rail station	✋ Admission charges: Expensive (over £9) Moderate (£6–£9), and Inexpensive (under £6)
Ⓜ Nearest Metro (subway) station	
🚌 Nearest bus route	

This guide is divided into four sections

● **Essential Edinburgh:** An introduction to the city and tips on making the most of your stay.

● **Edinburgh by Area:** We've broken the city into four areas, and recommended the best sights, shops, entertainment venues, nightlife and places to eat in each one. Suggested walks help you to explore on foot.

● **Where to Stay:** The best hotels, whether you're looking for luxury, budget or something in between.

● **Need to Know:** The info you need to make your trip run smoothly, including getting about by public transport, weather tips, emergency phone numbers and useful websites.

Navigation In the Edinburgh by Area chapter, we've given each area its own color, which is also used on the locator maps throughout the book and the map on the inside front cover.

Maps The fold-out map accompanying this book is a comprehensive street plan of Edinburgh. The grid on this fold-out map is the same as the grid on the locator maps within the book. We've given grid references within the book for each sight and listing.

Contents

Introducing Edinburgh

Edinburgh, Scotland's appealing capital city, attracts many thousands of visitors every year. They come for many reasons: to seek their ancestral roots, to experience the Festival or just to get a taste of what makes Scotland tick.

Few first-time visitors are prepared for the sheer majesty of the city and the richness of its history and culture. Edinburgh combines its past with all that's best in 21st-century life, making it a popular destination and a jumping-off point for exploring Scotland.

Reminders of the past are everywhere. The castle rises over the tall tenements, narrow streets and dark *vennels* (alleyways) of the Old Town, while, to the north, the broad streets and spacious squares of the New Town are lined with gracious 18th-century buildings. Look closer, though, and it becomes clear that the city is no time warp, a tourist hub existing as a living museum or theme park of the Enlightenment.

Scottish monarchs lived in Edinburgh as early as the 11th century, but the city did not become the royal capital until the reign of King James II (*r.* 1437–60). Political power moved to London with the Act of Union in 1707, but the Scotland Act of 1998 created a devolved Scottish Parliament, sitting in a dramatic building at Holyrood. The economy is dominated by the service sector, with the emphasis on financial services, which has encouraged growing numbers of young, ambitious, highly paid professionals. It's these people, rather than the visitors, who have charged the city's renaissance, turning the capital into a slick and stylish metropolis, whose quality of life is rated among the highest in the UK.

Take time to participate in some of the pleasures enjoyed by local people—plays, music, bar-hopping and the club scene—rather than a steady diet of tartan-obsessed Caledonian entertainment.

FACTS AND FIGURES

● The population of Edinburgh is around half a million. This swells to more than one million during the Festival in August.
● Together, Edinburgh's Old Town and New Town contain more than 4,500 listed buildings.
● The highest point is Arthur's Seat.
● The Water of Leith is the city's longest waterway at 35km (22 miles).

FIRE, FIRE

Edinburgh was the first city in the world to have a municipal fire service. It was founded in 1824 by local man James Braidwood (1800–61), who was recognized for his heroism in tackling raging fires of that year in High Street. He later moved to London, forming the precursor to the London Fire Brigade, but was killed in the Tooley Street fire.

FESTIVAL TIME

Edinburgh's Festival is not one event but many, running concurrently in August. The most prestigious is the Edinburgh International Festival, founded in 1947, which showcases world-class performing arts events. Side by side with this heavy-weight, the anarchic and vast Fringe has plays, music, comedy and dance in nearly 300 venues.

MILITARY TATTOO

Book early for this one. The spectacle, held on the castle Esplanade with military precision—the swirl of the kilts, the skirling of the pipes—is the greatest tattoo of them all (tickets: ☎ 0131 225 1188; edintattoo.co.uk). It takes place Monday–Saturday evenings for three weeks in August. At other times of the year, get an insight at the visitor center.

A Short Stay in Edinburgh

DAY 1

Morning Most popular is a stroll down the **Royal Mile** (▷ 28–29). Those who don't want to walk can take the **hop-on-hop-off bus** (▷ 119) to visit the major sights. Get to **Edinburgh Castle** (▷ 24–25) at opening time to avoid the crowds. Close by is the **Camera Obscura** (▷ 32). Take a bit of time to explore the alleyways (*vennels* and *wynds*) as you walk away from the castle along Castlehill.

Mid-morning Take a look on the right at Victoria Street, with its specialist shops. If you want to walk farther, continue onto West Bow and out into the attractive **Grassmarket** (▷ 32–33), with lots of opportunities for coffee. Retrace your steps and continue along the Royal Mile into Lawnmarket and along to High Street. Take a look at **St. Giles' Cathedral** (▷ 30).

Lunch Have lunch at **The Mitre** (▷ 43), diagonally opposite the Tron.

Afternoon Continue on High Street, where you will find the **Museum of Childhood** (▷ 53) and **John Knox House** (▷ 60) opposite. Continue onto Canongate, with the **Museum of Edinburgh** (▷ 54–55) on the right and **Canongate Tolbooth** (▷ 50–51) on the left. As you near the end of the road you will see the dramatic **Scottish Parliament Building** (▷ 57) on the right and shortly afterwards the **Palace of Holyroodhouse** (▷ 58–59).

Dinner For old-fashioned charm at a price try the **Witchery by the Castle** (▷ 44). For a taste of France, head for **Petit Paris** (▷ 44).

Evening Just to the west of the Old Town you will find **Usher Hall** (▷ 41), where you can take in a classical concert. If clubbing is more your thing, try **Espionage** (▷ 40).

DAY 2

Morning Start at the Waverley Station end of **Princes Street** (▷ 74). You can then decide if you want to explore the shops along the famous road or those behind it. Those preferring art can visit the **Scottish National Gallery** (▷ 72–73), just beyond the **Scott Monument** (▷ 76). It is possible to take the free link bus from here to the other galleries.

Mid-morning Have a coffee at the gallery or try the **Forth Floor Restaurant** (▷ 84, panel) at Harvey Nichols, on **Multrees Walk** (▷ 79, panel), just to the north of Princes Street. You can then explore the other designer shops on The Walk.

Lunch Take a pub lunch on Rose Street, which once boasted the most pubs of any street in Edinburgh. The **Mussel Inn** (▷ 85) is a good choice for seafood lovers.

Afternoon Catch a bus from Princes Street out to **Leith** (▷ 92–93) and visit the **Royal Yacht** *Britannia* (▷ 95) and the Ocean Terminal Centre if you fancy a bit of shopping. Take a walk along The Shore, with its trendy bars and smart restaurants.

Dinner Back in New Town, eat on the popular George Street. Try the Italian **Gusto** (▷ 85) or, for smart dining, the **Dome** (▷ 84).

Evening Still on George Street, try the most fashionable clubs **Lulu** (▷ 82) or **Shanghai** (▷ 82) in the boutique hotels Tigerlily and Le Monde. Try the Omni Centre at Greenside Place on Leith Street for cinema or a comedy show, or the **Edinburgh Playhouse** (▷ 81), a former cinema and now a multipurpose auditorium, for musicals, dance or rock concerts.

Top 25

TOP 25

▶ ▶ ▶

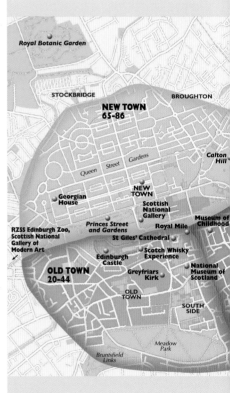

8

These pages are a quick guide to the Top 25, which are
described in more detail later. Here they are listed alphabeti-
cally, and the tinted background shows which area they are in.

Craigmillar Castle
▷ **90–91** A trip out to this
castle makes a pleasant
change from city bustle.

Edinburgh Castle
▷ **24–25** A million visitors
a year come to Scotland's
most famous castle.

Georgian House ▷ **69** ▼▼▼
The epitome of 18th-
century New Town elegance
is well worth a visit.

Greyfriars Kirk ▷ **26**
Lots of elaborate memorials
and the most famous of all,
Greyfriars Bobby.

Holyrood Park ▷ **52**
Take a walk on the wild side
in this pleasant park.

Leith ▷ **92–93**
Edinburgh's seaport and
now a trendy tourist area.

Museum of Childhood
▷ **53** Nostalgia and fun
abound in this museum for
big and little kids.

Museum of Edinburgh
▷ **54–55** A treasure house
of information and objects
all about Edinburgh.

**National Museum
of Scotland** ▷ **27**
An entertaining
introduction to Scottish
history and culture.

New Town ▷ **70–71**
18th-century planning at its
best—a prime example of
Georgian architecture.

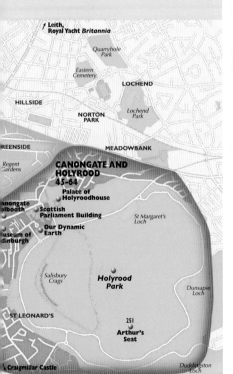

Leith,
Royal Yacht *Britannia*

Quarryhole
Park

Eastern
Cemetery

LOCHEND

HILLSIDE

NORTON
PARK

Lochend
Park

REENSIDE

MEADOWBANK

Regent
Gardens

**CANONGATE AND
HOLYROOD
45–64**
**Palace of
Holyroodhouse**

anongate
olbooth

**Scottish
Parliament Building**

St Margaret's
Loch

useum of
dinburgh

**Our Dynamic
Earth**

Salisbury
Crags

*Holyrood
Park*

Dunsapie
Loch

ST LEONARD'S

251
**Arthur's
Seat**

Craigmillar Castle

Duddingston
Loch

**Princes Street and
Gardens** ▷ **74** After
shopping in this famous
street, relax in the gardens.

Palace of Holyroodhouse
▷ **58–59** A royal palace rich
with historical associations
and works of art.

Our Dynamic Earth
▷ **56** Fun science with
great effects and
interactive enjoyment.

◀ ◀ ◀

Shopping

Edinburgh attracts shoppers from all over
the world, some looking for designer
styles, others hunting authentically Scottish
antiques, arts and crafts, cashmere and
tartan or fine whiskies.

Get Off the Beaten Track

Chain stores and souvenir outlets line Princes
Street and much of the Royal Mile, while
designer names like Boss and Louis Vuitton
dominate Multrees Walk and George Street.
For quirkier, more individual shopping, seek out
vintage stores, small galleries and idiosyncratic
design boutiques on the medieval Grassmarket,

villagey Stockbridge, trendy Broughton Street or
William Street in the West End. Edinburgh's
main museums and galleries sell books, ceramics, jewelry, textiles and prints inspired by their
collections. Fans of sword and sorcery epics and
movies like *Braveheart* and *Rob Roy* will find
accurate replicas of Highland dirks and broadswords alongside fantasy weaponry in several
specialist stores in the Old Town.

Edinburgh has always been a literary city, so
bibliophiles will find a better-than-average
selection of antiquarian and independent book-
shops specializing in everything from art and
Scottish history to fantasy and science fiction.

Made in Scotland

If you're looking for something typically Scottish,
you'll be spoiled for choice whatever your
budget. Woolens, tartans, tweeds and

From traditional to wacky,
designer to vintage—
Edinburgh has it all

MARKETS

Sunday sees thousands of locals heading out to Ingliston,
which is home to a huge, cheap and vibrant outdoor
market with more than 100 stands and a car boot sale
thrown in. Undercover markets include the rambling
New Street Sunday Market in Old Town. For the best
in Scottish produce, the Saturday Farmers' Market
(9–2), held on Castle Terrace, is worth a trawl for
superb organic meat, vegetables and other foods
(edinburghfarmersmarket.co.uk).

cashmeres are everywhere, and smaller stores sell designer knitted goods in rainbow hues, or tartan with a twist, bringing Scottish style right into the 21st century. Tartan can be found in the form of everything from a blanket to a kilt. Local craftspeople are celebrated for their silver, metalwork and jewelry, and you'll find samples at the swanky city stores or among dozens of tiny studio-workshops. You can find the country's musical heritage in a huge range of CDs—everything from reels and pipe-and-drum music to Celtic rock and traditional Gaelic song. Books, posters and calendars make great souvenirs and gifts, and you'll find an excellent selection here. Edinburgh is also well endowed with expensive antiques shops and fine art and contemporary galleries. Urban sophisticates can bypass all this to focus on furniture and objets d'art that combine traditional craftsmanship with cutting-edge design, not just from Scotland but from all over the world.

A Taste of Scotland

Food is always a popular souvenir, and shops sell the best of the country's produce, often vacuum-packed to make transportation easier. Choose from wild smoked salmon, Orkney cheese, heather honey and soft fruit jam, shortbread, oatcakes, superb cheeses and a bottle of the finest malt whisky from the huge range you'll find, some of which are 100 years old.

SHOPPING AREAS

The city's retail heart beats in Princes Street, and if you're looking for chain stores it's the best choice; if not, with the exception of the excellent department store Jenners, it can be avoided. For souvenirs, head for the Old Town, where tartan, tat, sweaters and whisky crowd the shelves. The New Town's best shops are around Queen Street, with big-name, classy shopping at Multrees Walk (▷ 79) off St. Andrew's Square—home to the beautiful Harvey Nichols. For good local shops, head for Stockbridge, Bruntsfield and Morningside. For style, William Street, in the city's West End, has some great specialist shops.

Shopping by Theme

Whether you're looking for a department store, a quirky boutique, or something in between, you'll find it all in Edinburgh. On this page shops are listed by theme. For a more detailed write-up, see the individual listings in Edinburgh by Area.

Edinburgh by Night

In summer the city fairly buzzes with all the activities of the festivals and their fringes, catering for every taste and budget. However, there's plenty to do at any time of the year.

Music, Theater, Dance and Film

Outside the Festival, Edinburgh has a year-round schedule of the performing arts, with plays, music, opera, dance, ballet, comedy, folk music, rock and jazz all on offer, while cinemas show blockbusters and art-house movies. You can find listings information in *The List*, a fortnightly magazine that details every type of entertainment. Tickets for major performances can be booked through Ticketmaster (ticketmaster.co.uk) in the VisitScotland office (3 Princes Street, Mon–Sat 9–5, Sun 10–5) or at venues.

Calmer Pleasures

If you're looking for a quieter evening, the city looks fantastic after dark, with many landmark buildings illuminated. Except for the Festival weeks, restaurants in Edinburgh tend to wind down around 10pm, so don't expect to find much open later; eat around 8pm, then head for a stylish bar or traditional pub.

Dance the Night Away

Edinburgh's clubs are far more subdued than those of Glasgow, London or Manchester and, as in many other cities, are often in a state of flux, with venues and clubs changing from one month to the next. Friday and Saturday are the big nights, when admission prices rise and places stay open later. Check out *The List* or the free sheet *Metro,* available Monday to Saturday.

Edinburgh is full of opportunities for classical, traditional or trendy nights out

HOGMANAY

Hogmanay is Scotland's New Year, and Edinburgh celebrates it in style with a four-day spectacle that includes concerts, street parties, live music, marching bands, processions and spectacular fireworks. Tickets go on sale in July from edinburghshogmanay.com.

Where to Eat

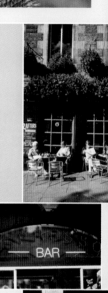

The culinary explorer is spoiled for choice in cosmopolitan Edinburgh. You don't have to look hard for traditional Scottish cuisine, but there are plenty of alternatives to be found, from Thai and Indian to Turkish and Moroccan.

Where and When to Eat

Restaurants reflect the diversity of British culture and there are options to suit most tastes and pockets. Some of the city's more formal restaurants are open only for lunch and dinner, but you can find somewhere to eat in Edinburgh from as early as 9am until midnight and even later. Many city center pubs serve unpretentious, decent meals all day. Many top restaurants are based in hotels, but you don't need to be staying at the hotel to enjoy the cuisine, although it is best to book in advance. Traditional tea shops are excellent for snacks and are usually open from mid-morning until 4 or 5pm. There are some good options in the larger department stores for light lunches and tea and coffee breaks.

International Dining

Ambitious, innovative cooking based on locally sourced produce and traditional recipes is easy to find, but Edinburgh also offers a good range of international restaurants, including long-established Italian trattorias. With the influx of Italian immigrants to Scotland in the early 20th century, you will find good pasta and, of course, the quintessential Italian-made ice cream.

Scotland's fresh produce can often be sampled outside as well as indoors

SCOTTISH SELECTION

Arbroath smokies—small hot-smoked haddock.
clootie dumpling—steamed sweet-and-spicy pudding, traditionally cooked in a cloth.
cranachan—raspberries, cream and toasted oatmeal.
crowdie—light curd cheese.
Cullen skink—creamy fish broth based on "Finnan haddie," or smoked haddock.
Forfar bridie—pasty made with beef, onion and potato.

Where to Eat by Cuisine

There are plenty of places to eat to suit all tastes and budgets in Edinburgh. On this page they are listed by cuisine. For a more detailed description of each restaurant, see Edinburgh by Area.

Top Tips For…

These great suggestions will help you tailor your ideal visit to Edinburgh, no matter how you choose to spend your time. Each suggestion has a fuller write-up elsewhere in the book.

SCOTTISH SOUVENIRS

Kilts and all things tartan can be found at Geoffrey (Tailor) Kiltmakers (▷ 62) and their Tartan Weaving Mill, right by the castle.

Scottish shortbread and fudge are sold at Cranachan & Crowdie (▷ 62).

Try a wee dram—there's a huge choice of Scotland's national tipple at Royal Mile Whiskies (▷ 39).

See the work of local craftspeople at Just Scottish (▷ 39).

For quality reproductions of prints, paintings, jewelry and other relics from the collections held in Edinburgh's great museums and art galleries, visit the shops in the National Museum of Scotland, the Scottish National Portrait Gallery or the National Library of Scotland.

Superior malt whisky makes a great gift

LUXURIOUS CASHMERE

Belinda Robertson (▷ 78) produces designer cashmere products to dress the stars.

For the very best quality shop at Hawico (▷ 38), but it will cost.

SCOTTISH FOOD

Enjoy top dining and Scottish classics with a contemporary twist at the Witchery (▷ 44).

Sample top Scottish cuisine at Dubh Prais Restaurant (▷ 64), with everything from haggis to venison and salmon.

Try the Whiski Rooms (▷ 44) on the Royal Mile for hundreds of malt whiskies and a menu that emphasizes locally produced meat, game and seafood.

A taste of luxury, be it supersoft cashmere (middle) or delicious locally caught salmon (bottom)

When the weather's good, eat outside or take to the hills

INTERNATIONAL COOKING

Cool, sleek and Italian is the dish of the day at Gusto (▷ 85).

French cuisine in Grassmarket—try a delightful country-style bistro in the heart of the city at Petit Paris (▷ 44).

Dine on fresh seafood at the Mussel Inn (▷ 85), simply prepared and a delight to the taste buds.

A taste of South Asia can be found at Dishoom (▷ 84) on St. Andrew Square.

A BREATH OF FRESH AIR

Classical Edinburgh can be found at the top of Calton Hill (▷ 68).

For some salty air head out to Leith (▷ 92–93) and go aboard the Royal Yacht *Britannia* (▷ 95).

In the heart of the city stroll in the delightful Princes Street Gardens (▷ 74).

If you are feeling energetic get down to Holyrood Park (▷ 52) and climb up to Arthur's Seat (▷ 48–49).

Walking the dog on Calton Hill

BOUTIQUE HOTELS

Stay in a historic New Town building in glamorous 12 Picardy Place (▷ 110), superbly located just off York Place.

Enjoy spectacular views of Calton Hill from the comfort of your bedroom at the Glasshouse (▷ 112).

One of the coolest hotels in town is The Bonham (▷ 112), nicely located in New Town.

True elegance and sophistication can be found at The Howard (▷ 112).

Relax in one of Edinburgh's newest boutique hotels

Attractions in the city range from art to animals

SAVING MONEY

Buy day tickets for 24 hours of unlimited central zone bus and tram travel (▷ 118).
Try the all-you-can-eat Chinese banquet at Chop Chop (▷ 106).
The National Museum of Scotland (▷ 27) and the Scottish National Gallery (▷ 72–73) are both free and packed with treasures.
Picnic in the park at Princes Street Gardens (▷ 74) in the city center or the Royal Botanic Garden (▷ 94).

A KID'S DAY OUT

See the animals at the world-renowned zoo (▷ 96–97).
Give yourself a scare in the Edinburgh Dungeon (▷ 75).
Be hands-on and scientific at the terrific Our Dynamic Earth (▷ 56).
It's free at the Museum of Childhood (▷ 53).

SOME ACTION

Play a round of golf just outside the city (▷ 105, panel).
Enjoy a swim at the Royal Commonwealth Pool (▷ 105).
See Scottish football at Hearts or Hibs (▷ 105).
Spend a day at the races—check out the horses at Musselburgh Racecourse (▷ 105).

The game of golf began in Scotland

GOING OUT ON THE TOWN

Traditional music can be found at Sandy Bells Bar (▷ 40, panel).
Go clubbing at Lulu (▷ 82), in the trendy Tigerlily hotel.
Boogie all night at club Espionage (▷ 40).
Some great jazz, soul and blues bands appear at The Jazz Bar (▷ 41).

Take to the dance floor

The essence of old Edinburgh can be found in this district, with its narrow alleys, ancient *wynds* and compact lanes. The Old Town sees the start of the Royal Mile, dominated by the impressive castle.

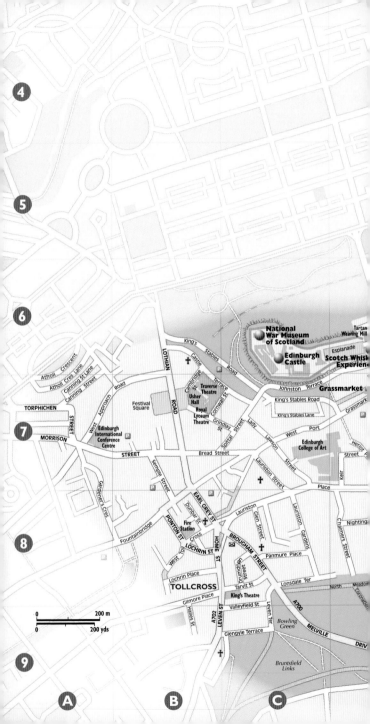

4

5

6

National
War Museum
of Scotland

Tartan
Weaving Mill

Edinburgh
Castle

Esplanade

Scotch Whisk
Experien

King's Stables Road

Johnston Terrace

Grassmarket

Athol
Crescent

Athol Cres Lane

Canning St Lane

Canning street

Cambridge St

Castle Terrace

King's Stables Road

King's Stables Lane

Grassmark

LOTHIAN ROAD

West Approach Road

Festival
Square

Traverse
Theatre

Usher
Hall

Royal
Lyceum
Theatre

Cornwall St

Grindlay St

Lady Lawson Street

West Port

Edinburgh
College of Art

Heriot

Street

TORPHICHEN

STREET

7

MORRISON

Edinburgh
International
Conference
Centre

Spittal Street

STREET

Bread Street

Laurison Street

Place

Keir

Gardner's Cres

Semple Street

EARL GREY ST

Dunbar St

Lauriston Street

Glen Street

Laurison Gardens

Chalmers Street

Nighting

8

Fountainbridge

PONTON ST

HOME ST

Fire
Station

LOCHRIN ST

West

Cross

BROUGHAM STREET

Drummond Street

Panmure Place

Lochrin Place

TOLLCROSS

Tarvit St

Lonsdale Ter

North

Meado

Gilmore Place

Hailles St

LEVEN ST

Valleyfield St

King's Theatre

Leven Ter

A700

MELVILLE

Bowling
Green

DRIV

Glengyle Terrace

Bruntsfield
Links

0 — 200 m
0 — 200 yds

9

A   **B**   **C**

The Real Mary
King's Close
Cockburn St

The Writers'
Museum

Mercat
Cross

Royal
Mile

The Mound

iladstone's
Land

Lawnmarket

High Street

Blair St

SOUTH BRIDGE

Camera
Obscura
& World
of Illusions

Victoria St

Heart of
Midlothian

St Giles' Cathedral

Charles II
Statue

George IV Bridge

Parliament House

Cowgate

National
Library of
Scotland

Guthrie St

University of
Edinburgh Old College

Talbot Rice
Gallery

Candlemaker Row

OLD
TOWN

Bristol Bridge

Heriot Bridge

Chambers Street

National
Museum of
Scotland

Surgeons' Hall
Museums

NICOLSON STREET

Greyfriars
Kirk

Forrest Rd

Bristo Place

Bedlam
Theatre

Teviot Pl

Potterrow

Festival
Theatre

Nicolson Square

Bristo
Square

Windmill
Street

Mosque

West Nicolson Street

Lauriston Place

University of
Edinburgh

Chapel Street

Way

George Street

P

Simpson Loan

George square

SOUTH
SIDE

George Square
Gardens

University of
Edinburgh

CLERK STREET

St Patrick St

Buccleuch St

Meadow
Park

George Square

Buccleuch Place

George Square Lane

Meadow Lane

Buccleuch Street

Gifford
Place

Jawbone Walk

Middle Meadow Walk

Boys Brigade Walk

North
Tennis
Courts

Meadow

Walk

Hope
Park Ter

SOUTH CLERK STREET

MELVILLE

DRIVE

A700

SUMMERHILL PLACE

D   **E**   **F**   **G**

Edinburgh Castle

HIGHLIGHTS

- Great views
- St. Margaret's Chapel
- Mons Meg
- Prisons of War Exhibition
- Scottish Crown Jewels
- Stone of Destiny
- One O'Clock Gun

TIP

- The nearest car parking zones are at Castle Terrace and Johnston Terrace. Visitors with disabilities can park at the castle (reserve ahead ☎ 0131 310 5114).

Perched high on a wedge of volcanic rock, the castle is a symbol of the Scottish nation, reflecting 1,000 years of history in a mix of architectural styles.

Might and majesty As you wind your way up the Castle Rock you can enjoy the view north over the city. The cannons along the battery were a picturesque improvement suggested by Queen Victoria, while the One O'Clock Gun, a field gun from World War II, fires from Mills Mount Battery at precisely 1pm. To enter the castle you first cross the Esplanade, the setting for the annual Military Tattoo (▷ 5).

Once inside The oldest structure in the castle is the 12th-century chapel, dedicated to St. Margaret by her son, David I. The chapel is

Clockwise from far left: full military pageant at the annual Edinburgh Tattoo, staged at the castle; stained-glass window depicting Queen Margaret inside St. Margaret's Chapel; the proud fortress overlooks the city; St. Margaret's Chapel; bands at the Tattoo; Mons Meg cannon on the ramparts

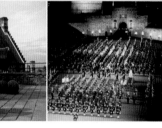

almost overshadowed by the huge cannon on the rampart outside—Mons Meg, a gift in 1457 to James II from the Duke of Burgundy, who wished to support the Scots against the English.

Castle of contrasts Be prepared for crowds in the Crown Room, where the Scottish Crown Jewels and the Stone of Destiny are displayed. The crown, dating from 1540, is made of Scottish gold, studded with semiprecious stones from the Cairngorms. The sword and scepter were papal gifts. The Stone of Destiny was the stone on which Scottish kings were crowned—pinched by Edward I, it was recovered from London's Westminster Abbey in 1996. The castle also contains the National War Museum of Scotland (▷ 34), the Scottish War Memorial and the Prisons of War Exhibition.

THE BASICS

edinburghcastle.gov.uk

✚ C6

✉ Castlehill EH1 2NG

☎ 0131 225 9846

🕐 Apr–Sep daily 9.30–6; Oct–Mar daily 9.30–5

🍴 Cafés

🚌 23, 27, 41, 42

♿ Some areas are restricted; call first. A courtesy minibus takes less mobile people to the top of the castle site—check when you buy your ticket

💷 Expensive

Greyfriars Kirk

TOP 25

The loyal Greyfriars Bobby sits patiently outside the church and graveyard

THE BASICS

greyfriarskirk.com

✚ E7

✉ Greyfriars Tolbooth and Highland Kirk, Greyfriars Place EH1 2QQ

☎ 0131 225 1900

🕐 Apr–Oct Mon–Fri 10.30–4.30, Sat 10.30–2.30; Nov–Mar Thu 1.30–3.30

🚌 2, 23, 27, 35, 41, 42

♿ Very good

🎫 Free

HIGHLIGHTS

● Greyfriars Bobby
● Elaborate 17th-century memorials
● Peaceful surroundings
● Gaelic service held at 12.30 on Sunday, when all are welcome

Built in 1620 on the site of the garden of a former Franciscan monastery, the Kirk of the Grey Friars has had a turbulent history. Today it is a peaceful haven for quiet contemplation.

Battleground Just 18 years after the church was built, it was the scene of a pivotal event in Scottish history, when Calvinist petitioners gathered to sign the National Covenant, an act of defiance against the king, Charles I. The church itself was trashed by Cromwell's troops in 1650, and later accidentally blown up. In the kirkyard a makeshift prison was erected to house hundreds of Covenanters captured after the battle of Bothwell Bridge in 1679; they were kept here for five dreadful months. Today it is full of elaborate memorials, including the grave of architect William Adam (1689–1748).

Undying loyalty Opposite the churchyard gate stands a popular Edinburgh landmark: a fountain with a bronze statue of a little Skye terrier, which has stood here since 1873. The dog's story was told by American Eleanor Atkinson in her 1912 novel *Greyfriars Bobby*. He was the devoted companion of a local farmer who dined regularly in Greyfriars Place. After his master died, Bobby slept on his grave in the nearby churchyard for 14 years. A later version suggests he was owned by a local policeman, and taken in by local residents when his owner died. There is a portrait of Bobby, painted by John MacLeod in 1867, inside the church.

The striking National Museum of Scotland incorporates the former Royal Museum

National Museum of Scotland

Side by side, a splendid 19th-century building and an equally impressive modernist tower that tips its hat to Scotland's baronial architecture house treasures that span millennia.

Much to see With 10 new galleries that opened in 2016, the museum embraces every aspect of Scotland's natural and human history, heritage and geography. Plan to spend at least half a day here. To keep you going, there's a good café at street level and the outstanding Tower restaurant on the top floor.

The highlights The modern wing houses Pictish symbol-stones, Roman and Viking silver, Norse and Celtic rings, pins and brooches, chess pieces carved from walrus ivory, Jacobite silver and modern sculpture. Don't miss the first-century Hunterston brooch, the beautiful 8th-century Monymusk Reliquary or the mysterious miniature coffins, each containing a tiny human effigy, discovered on Arthur's Seat in 1836. Look out too for the skeleton of a Viking noble who was buried with his tools, weapons and valuables in Orkney more than 1,000 years ago. His teeth are in surprisingly good condition.

The new galleries The renovated 19th-century wing houses an eclectic collection, ranging from skeletons of whales and dinosaurs to early aircraft, racing cars and computers. The interactive technology zone between the two wings will keep kids of all ages entertained.

THE BASICS

nms.ac.uk

➕ E7

✉ Chambers Street EH1 1JF

☎ 0300 123 6789

🕐 Daily 10–5

🍴 Tower restaurant (▷ 44); reservations essential at weekends. Museum Brasserie

🚌 2, 23, 27, 35, 41, 42

♿ Very good

🎟 Free; charge for some temporary exhibitions

❓ Check on arrival for times of free daily tours. Free audio guides available in English, Gaelic, French, Spanish, Italian and German

HIGHLIGHTS

● Pictish carvings
● Hunterston brooch
● Lewis chess pieces
● Robbie Burns' pistols
● Eduardo Paolozzi sculptures
● Great views from the roof

OLD TOWN TOP 25

Royal Mile

Stretching down from Edinburgh Castle to Holyrood, the Royal Mile is a focal point for visitors, who can explore the narrow *wynds* leading off the main thoroughfare.

Origins The Royal Mile is the long, almost straight street leading up the spine of rock on which the Old Town was built. Lined with medieval tenement houses, this part of the city became so overcrowded that a New Town (▷ 70–71) was built in the 18th century. About 60 narrow closes, or *wynds,* lead off it on either side, whose names, such as Fleshmarket, indicate the trades once carried out there.

Down to earth The Scottish Parliament (▷ 57) dominates the Holyrood end of the Royal Mile. From here, the area around

Clockwise from top left: Deacon Brodie's—a traditional pub on the Royal Mile; tartan for sale at shops along the Mile; striking Old Town houses at the back of the Royal Mile; the official Royal Mile sign; on the Lawnmarket; attractive pub sign for Deacon Brodie's; buildings on Cockburn Street

Canongate developed into a more practical, working district. Visit the Museum of Edinburgh (▷ 54–55) for a glimpse of the interiors of these old houses. Look for a board outside Canongate Kirk that lists the famous people buried there.

Onward and upward At the crossing of St. Mary's Street and Jeffrey Street you enter High Street. After St. Giles' Cathedral (▷ 30), with the Heart of Midlothian (▷ 33) in the cobbles, the street becomes the Lawnmarket, with its fine 16th- and 17th-century tenements where linen (lawn) was manufactured. On the final stretch above the Hub (a former church that is now headquarters of the Edinburgh Festival) the road narrows on the steep approach to the castle (▷ 24–25).

THE BASICS

➕ C6–H5
✉ The Royal Mile
🚌 23, 27, 35, 41, 42

TIP

● The route has four sections, each with its own identity. You may wish to walk it all in one go or choose to concentrate on one part.

St. Giles' Cathedral

Striking stained glass depicting biblical scenes in St. Giles' Cathedral

THE BASICS

stgilescathedral.org.uk

✚ E6

✉ High Street EH1 1RE

☎ 0131 226 0674

🕐 May–Sep Mon–Fri 9–7, Sat 9–5, Sun 1–5; Oct–Apr Mon–Sat 9–5, Sun 1–5 (and for services year-round)

🍴 St. Giles' Cathedral Café

🚌 23, 27, 35, 41, 42

♿ Very good

🎟 Free. A donation of £3 is invited

HIGHLIGHTS

● Robert Louis Stevenson memorial
● Window designed by Edward Burne-Jones
● Robert Burns window
● Stained glass
● John Knox statue
● Medieval stonework

Imposing, and its dark stonework somewhat forbidding, the High Kirk of Edinburgh stands near the top of the Royal Mile. It is dedicated to St. Giles, the patron saint of the city.

Origins of the building The columns inside the cathedral that support the 49m (160ft) tower, with its distinctive crown top, are a relic of the 12th-century church that once occupied this site. The tower itself dates from 1495, and is one of the few remaining examples of 15th-century work to be seen in High Street today. Much of the church has been reworked over subsequent centuries. Don't miss the exquisitely carved 19th-century Thistle Chapel.

Saintly beginnings St. Giles' parish church—it became a cathedral in the mid-17th century—was probably founded by Benedictine followers of Giles. He was a 7th-century hermit (and later abbot and saint) who lived in France, a country with strong ties to Scotland. In 1466, the Preston Aisle of the church was completed, in memory of William Preston, who had acquired the arm bone of the saint in France. This relic disappeared in about 1577, but St. Giles' other arm bone is still in St. Giles' Church, Bruges.

Famous sons Presbyterian reformer John Knox (c.1513–72) became minister here in 1559. You can also see a bronze memorial to writer Robert Louis Stevenson (1850–94), who died in Samoa.

Scotch Whisky Experience

After you've learned about Scotland's national drink, you can try it for yourself

This first-class visitor attraction has matured well since opening in 1988. Now a £2 million refurbishment offers new features and a fresh approach, creating the perfect blend for the 21st century.

On the whisky trail Take a barrel ride and become part of the whisky-making process. You journey through fields of gently swaying barley and on to the warmth of the Malt Kiln, with its lingering smell of burning peat. Next stop is the Malt Mill, followed by the Mash Tun. Then it's off to the turbulent wooden Washback, with the sound of the sloshing Wash, before the steaming Pot Still. Breathe in the smell of the Oak Casks as the process slows down to the tick-tock of the years of maturation.

Whisky brought to life Characters in costume tell the stories behind the amber liquid and guide you through its development. In the vault you can view the Diageo Claive Vidiz Scotch Whisky Collection, the world's largest collection of Scotch whiskies, and experience the age-old art of "nosing," enabling you to decide if you like fruity, sweet or smoky flavors and to select your perfect dram. The tour concludes with an exhibition charting the humble origins of whisky through to the drink's global success today. Then you can choose from more than 300 types of whisky and liqueurs in the bar.

Too young to drink? Children can enjoy a tour led by Peat, the distillery cat.

THE BASICS

scotchwhiskyexperience.co.uk

🔲 D6

✉ 354 Castlehill, The Royal Mile EH1 2NE

☎ 0131 220 0441

🕐 Apr–Jul daily 10–6; Aug Mon–Fri 10–5, Sat–Sun 10–6; Sep–Mar daily 10–5

🍴 Amber Restaurant (▷ 42)

🚌 23, 27, 41, 42

♿ Very good

💷 Expensive

HIGHLIGHTS

● Barrel ride
● World's largest collection of Scottish whiskies
● Tasting a dram of your choice
● Children's and specialist tours

More to See

CAMERA OBSCURA AND WORLD OF ILLUSIONS

camera-obscura.co.uk

At the top of the Royal Mile a castellated building known as the Outlook Tower offers five floors of interactive optical experiences from illusions to holograms. On the top floor is the camera obscura itself, invented in the 19th century, and like a giant pin-hole camera; it doesn't use film but projects onto a viewing table a fascinating panorama of the city outside (visit on a clear day).

🞢 D6 ✉ Castlehill EH1 2ND ☎ 0131 226 3709 🕐 Jul–Aug daily 9–9; Apr–Jun, Sep–Oct 9.30–7; Nov–Mar 10–6 🚌 23, 27, 41, 42 ♿ None 💷 Expensive

CHARLES II STATUE

This splendid memorial to King Charles II (1630–85) is the oldest statue in the city and the oldest equestrian statue in Britain. Made of lead, it was erected in 1685, but the sculptor is unknown.

🞢 E6 ✉ Parliament Square 🚌 23, 27, 35

GLADSTONE'S LAND

nts.org.uk

This restored 17th-century tenement is a highlight in the Old Town. It emphasizes the cramped Old Town conditions—the only space for expansion was up. The building's eventual height of six floors reflects the status of its merchant owner, Thomas Gledstanes, who extended the existing tenement in 1617. The National Trust for Scotland has re-created 17th-century shop-booths on the ground floor.

🞢 D6 ✉ 477b Lawnmarket EH1 2NT ☎ 0131 226 5856 🕐 Late Mar–Oct daily 10–5 🚌 23, 27, 41, 42, 45 ♿ Few; phone for details 💷 Moderate

GRASSMARKET

A long open space below the castle rock, the Grassmarket was first chartered as a market in 1477. It was also the site of public executions. A stone marks the location of the old gibbet and commemorates the Covenanting martyrs who died

Guarding the entrance to Gladstone's Land

Victoria Street, off Grassmarket

here. Smartened up in recent years, it now has many good shops and eating places, including the ancient White Hart Inn.

🞦 D7 ✉ Grassmarket 🚌 2, 35, 41

HEART OF MIDLOTHIAN

With your back to the entrance of St. Giles' Cathedral, move 20 paces forward and slightly to the right, look down and you will see the out-line of a heart in the cobblestones. This Heart of Midlothian marks the place of the old Tolbooth prison, where executions took place.

🞦 E6 ✉ High Street EH1 1RE 🚌 35, 42

MEADOW PARK

Known as the Meadows, this area of paths and tree-planted areas make an ideal place to wander away from the hustle of the city—although not such a good place to be at night. Students, doctors and nurses from the Royal Infirmary and local families all mingle here.

🞦 D8 ✉ Meadow Park 🚌 3, 3A, 5, 7, 31 ♿ Good

MERCAT CROSS

Located outside St. Giles' Cathedral, the cross was traditionally the location for public declarations, gatherings and executions. The present version, dating from the 1880s, is fashioned on the 17th-century cross, although there may have been a cross here since the 12th century.

🞦 E6 ✉ High Street 🚌 23, 27, 35, 41, 42

NATIONAL LIBRARY OF SCOTLAND

nls.uk

This dignified building houses extensive collections of reference works, maps, fiction and non-fiction by Scottish authors and publishers and hosts a year-round calendar of literary exhibitions. Highlights include the John Murray Archive, a collection of thousands of manu-scripts, letters and other documents from authors including Jane Austen, Lord Byron, Charles Darwin and David Livingstone. The NLS also houses the Scottish Screen Archive,

The Heart of Midlothian

Mercat Cross

a collection of hundreds of moving images covering more than 100 years of Scottish cinematic history.

🟥 E6 ✉ George IV Bridge EH1 1EW
🎟 0131 623 3700 🕐 Mon–Tue, Thu–Fri 9.30–8.30, Wed 10–8, Sat 9.30–1 🚌 23, 27, 41, 42, 67 ♿ Good 💷 Free

NATIONAL WAR MUSEUM OF SCOTLAND

nms.ac.uk

Exploring more than 400 years of Scottish military history, this museum has displays ranging from major events in Scottish warfare to the personal—diaries, private photographs and belongings of ordinary soldiers. Highlights include a pipe given by a German soldier to a sergeant in the Scots Guards on Christmas Day 1914, weaponry, gallantry medals, and even three elephant's toes.

🟥 C6 ✉ Edinburgh Castle, Castle Hill EH1 2NG 🎟 0131 247 4413 🕐 Daily 9.45–5.45 (closes 4.45 Nov–Mar) 🚌 23, 27, 41, 42 ♿ Good 💷 Expensive (as part of ticket for castle)

PARLIAMENT HOUSE

Home to the law courts, this is the heart of the Scottish legal system. Dating from the 17th century, and restored in 2013, it has a fine hammerbeam roof and a 19th-century stained-glass window. It was home to Parliament from 1639 to 1707 and again after devolution between 1999 and 2004.

🟥 E6 ✉ Parliament Square EH1 1RQ
🎟 0131 225 2595 🕐 Mon–Fri 9–5 🚌 23, 27, 35, 41, 42 ♿ Good 💷 Free

THE REAL MARY KING'S CLOSE

realmarykingsclose.com

Remnants of the Old Town's 17th-century houses have been preserved beneath the City Chamber, which was built over the top in 1753. Guided tours underground bring the close and its people to life.

🟥 E6 ✉ 2 Warriston's Close, High Street EH1 1PG 🎟 0131 225 0672 🕐 Apr–Oct daily 10–9 (Aug 9–9); Nov–Mar Sun–Fri 10–5, Sat 10–9 🚌 23, 27, 35, 41, 42 ♿ Few; phone for details 💷 Expensive

Checking out the displays in the National War Museum of Scotland

Back in time at the Real Mary King's Close

SURGEONS' HALL MUSEUMS

museum.rcsed.ac.uk

Opened in 1832 on the campus of the Royal College of Surgeons when Edinburgh was at the cutting edge of medical science, Surgeons' Hall Museums is fascinating in a gruesome way. Exhibits include surgical instruments, bone and tissue specimens, one of the world's largest assortments of surgical pathology and a dental collection that will make your teeth twinge. The museum also highlights the criminal careers of Burke and Hare, who notoriously took to murder to make up for a shortfall in cadavers available to medical science in the 1820s.

🚩 F7 ✉ Nicolson Street EH8 9DW
📞 0131 527 1711 🕐 Daily 10–5 🚌 3, 7, 8, 14, 33 ♿ Good 💷 Moderate

TALBOT RICE GALLERY

ed.ac.uk/about/museums-galleries/talbot-rice

This gallery, within the University of Edinburgh, was established in 1975 and hosts changing exhibitions of the work of international artists and Scottish art. There is also the fine permanent Torrie collection of Dutch and Italian Old Masters.

🚩 E7 ✉ Old College, South Bridge EH8 9YL
📞 0131 650 2210 🕐 Open only for exhibitions 🚌 3, 7, 8, 14, 33 ♿ Good 💷 Free

THE WRITERS' MUSEUM

edinburghmuseums.org.uk

The 17th-century Lady Stair's House is home to The Writers' Museum and dedicated to Robert Burns (1759–96), Sir Walter Scott (1771–1832) and Robert Louis Stevenson (1850–94). Scott and Stevenson were both born in Edinburgh and studied law at the university. Particularly significant is Stevenson's memorabilia, as he died abroad and there is no other museum dedicated to him. Contemporary Scottish authors are also represented.

🚩 D6 ✉ Lady Stair's Close, Lawnmarket, Royal Mile EH1 2PA 📞 0131 529 4901
🕐 Mon–Sat 10–5; also Sun 12–5 in Aug
🚌 35 ♿ Phone for details 💷 Free

The Pathology Museum in the Surgeons' Hall Museums

Robert Burns memorabilia on display at The Writers' Museum

A Wander Around the Old Town

Take in some of the highlights off the beaten track and get a glimpse of the buildings of the Old Town.

DISTANCE: 2km (1 mile) **ALLOW:** 45 minutes (but more time with stops)

START

ST. GILES' CATHEDRAL
⊞ E6 🚌 23, 27, 35, 41

END

HIGH STREET
⊞ E6 🚌 35

OLD TOWN WALK

1 Start at the imposing St. Giles' Cathedral (▷ 30) on High Street, with the Mercat Cross (▷ 33) outside. With the cathedral to your left, take the next left over George IV bridge.

2 Also known as Melbourne Place, this will take you down to the National Museum of Scotland (▷ 27). Cross the road to Greyfriars, at the end of which is Greyfriars Kirk (▷ 26).

3 Turn down Candlemaker Row and keep bearing left until you come into Grassmarket (▷ 32–33).

4 You can divert here to the right for West Bow, which leads to Victoria Street for specialty shopping and cafés. Return to Grassmarket and look for St. Andrew's Cross.

8 Escape the crowds by wandering along some of the old narrow *wynds* (alleys). Continue along Lawnmarket and back to the High Street.

7 Take Granny Green's Steps up to the castle (▷ 24–25). Turn right and follow the castle along until you eventually come to the Hub, a redundant church with a high spire. Cross over into Lawnmarket to soak up the atmosphere of the Old Town.

6 At the bottom of Grassmarket, in the left-hand corner, take the Vennel, a series of steps up to the city wall, for a good view of the castle. Return to the Grassmarket and cross to the far corner.

5 This is railed and set into the cobbles and is the site of the old gallows.

Shopping

ARMSTRONGS

armstrongsvintage.co.uk

Established in 1840, museum-like Armstrongs is Scotland's largest vintage emporium, featuring sassy, retro and traditional Scottish clothing. There are also branches at 64–66 Clerk Street and 14 Teviot Place.

🔲 D7 ✉ 83 Grassmarket EH1 2HJ ☎ 0131 220 5557 🚍 2

BILL BABER

billbaber.com

Bill Baber and his partner Helen have been creating beautiful garments since 1977, using yarns of raw and blended silk, organic Irish linen and soft Egyptian cotton, as well as merino wool spun and dyed in Milan.

🔲 D7 ✉ 66 Grassmarket EH1 2JR ☎ 0131 225 3249 🚍 2, 23, 27, 41

CIGAR BOX

This Royal Mile retailer has achieved the Gold Standard in Habanos. From famous names like Montecristo and Romeo y Julieta to cigars from as far afield as Honduras and Nicaragua, you'll find them here.

🔲 E6 ✉ 361 High Street EH1 1PW ☎ 0131 225 3534 🚍 35 and North Bridge buses

---

SCOTTISH WOOL

If you're looking for the very best in Scottish woolens, you could easily spend a small fortune on designer cashmere in Edinburgh. However, there's also a plethora of factory outlets with good-quality knitwear at knockdown prices, particularly cashmere, although you are unlikely to find anything leading the way in designer fashion here. Serious knitters will delight in the huge range of yarns available in every conceivable shade, at a good price.

DEMIJOHN

demijohn.co.uk

Demijohn is a liquid deli where you can taste the products and personalize them with your choice of bottle. It sells liqueurs, spirits, whiskies, oils, vinegars and spices from around the world.

🔲 D6 ✉ 32 Victoria Street EH1 2JW ☎ 0131 225 4090 🚍 2, 23, 27, 41

FABHATRIX

fabhatrix.com

This hat shop promotes Scottish designers and many hats are made on the premises. You'll find everything from tweed to trendy fascinators.

🔲 D7 ✉ 13 Cowgatehead EH1 1JY ☎ 0131 225 9222 🚍 2, 23, 27, 41

HAWICO

hawico.com

Cashmere doesn't come cheap and sweaters from this boutique start at £180—the Cashmere Made In Scotland label attached to each garment satisfies that the clothes are of the highest quality. The scarves are less expensive.

🔲 D7 ✉ 71 Grassmarket EH1 2HJ ☎ 0131 225 8634 🚍 2

HERMAN BROWN

hermanbrown.co.uk

Just off Grassmarket, Herman Brown has a wealth of hand-picked vintage clothing and accessories.

🔲 C7 ✉ 151 West Port EH3 9DP ☎ 0131 228 2589 🚍 23, 27, 41, 42, 67

IAN MELLIS

mellischeese.net

The range of Scottish cheeses at this cheesemonger's is overwhelming, but staff will help find the perfect cheese for your palate. There are also branches in Morningside and Stockbridge.

D6 ✉ 30a Victoria Street EH1 2JW
☎ 0131 226 6215 🚌 2, 23, 27, 41

JUST SCOTTISH

justscottishart.com

Here you'll find an eclectic mix of fine
and applied art from Scotland's best artists. Choose from zany cushions,
traditional ceramics, beautifully crafted
wooden items and a selection of cards.

D6 ✉ 4–6 North Bank Street EH1 2LP
☎ 0131 226 4806 (gallery 0131 226 4807)
🚌 3, 3A, 31, 33

MR WOOD'S FOSSILS

mrwoodsfossils.co.uk

This shop originally supplied museums
but now specializes in selling fossils,
crystals and minerals from Scotland and
all over the world. Knowledgeable and
friendly staff will fill you in on Lizzie, the
oldest reptile ever discovered.

D7 ✉ 5 Cowgatehead EH1 1JY ☎ 0131
220 1344 🚌 2, 23, 27, 41, 42

OLD TOWN BOOKSHOP

oldtownbookshop-edinburgh.co.uk

Secondhand books on Scotland and
works by Scottish writers, plus music, art
and travel fill the shelves here, along
with a good range of prints and maps.

D6 ✉ 8 Victoria Street EH1 2HG ☎ 0131
225 9237 🚌 2, 23, 27, 41

RED DOOR GALLERY

edinburghart.com

This gallery sells original prints, quirky
accessories, jewelry and more.

D6 ✉ 42 Victoria Street EH1 2JW
☎ 0131 477 3255 🚌 23, 27, 41, 42, 67

ROYAL MILE ARMOURIES

heritageofscotland.com

With its impressive-looking replica
broadswords, daggers, battle-axes,

helmets and armor, this shop will bring
out your inner barbarian and delight
fans of *Braveheart*, *Game of Thrones*
and *The Lord of the Rings*.

D6 ✉ 555 Castle Hill EH1 2ND ☎ 0131
225 8580 🚌 23, 27, 41, 42, 67

ROYAL MILE WHISKIES

royalmilewhiskies.com

Enthusiasts are on hand to offer advice
on the hundreds of single malt whiskies
stocked here—some are 100 years old.
Have your items shipped home, or
order by phone or online.

E6 ✉ 379 High Street EH1 1PW ☎ 0131
524 9380 🚌 23, 27, 35, 41, 42

TRANSREAL FICTION

transreal.co.uk

This bookstore is a delight for lovers
of science fiction and fantasy. Fans of
well-known Edinburgh-based writers
like Ken MacLeod and Charles Stross
will find signed copies of their latest
works here.

E7 ✉ 46 Candlemaker Row EH1 2QE
☎ 0131 226 6266 🚌 2, 23, 27, 41

Entertainment and Nightlife

BEDLAM THEATRE

bedlamtheatre.co.uk

This 90-seat, student-run theater in a one-time Gothic church is home to Edinburgh University Theatre Company. It presents original and experimental works and is a popular Fringe venue.

➕ E7 ✉ 11 Bistro Place EH1 1EZ ☎ 0131 629 0430 🚌 23, 24, 27, 29, 41, 42, 45

CABARET VOLTAIRE

thecabaretvoltaire.com

Housed in old subterranean vaults in the Cowgate district, this club is a twin-roomed venue hosting some great gigs. You'll find all types of music, with some 30 live acts a month.

➕ E6 ✉ 36 Blair Street EH1 1QR ☎ 0131 247 4704 🕐 Nightly (check for times) 🚌 5, 7, 14, 29, 35, 37

CAMEO

picturehouses.co.uk

Cameo, one of the oldest cinemas in Scotland still in use, is a small, comfortable cinema showing the more thoughtful Hollywood hits, plus international and independent films.

CELTIC MUSIC

Edinburgh pubs and dinner shows are the best places to track down a genuine Celtic music session. Celtic music originates from the seven Celtic regions—Scotland, Ireland, Wales, Isle of Man, Cornwall, Brittany and Galicia. The following city pubs have fine singers and musicians performing on a regular basis: Sandy Bells Bar (✉ Forrest Road EH1 2QH ☎ 0131 225 2751); The Tass (✉ corner of High Street and St. Mary's Street EH1 1SR ☎ 0131 556 6338); The Royal Oak (✉ Infirmary Street EH1 1LT ☎ 0131 557 2976). Dates and times can be erratic—check first.

➕ B8 ✉ 38 Home Street EH3 9LZ 🚌 10, 11, 15, 16, 17, 23, 27, 37

EDINBURGH FESTIVAL THEATRE

edtheatres.com

This theater, with its distinctive glass facade outside and traditional sumptuous decor inside, has one of the largest stages in Europe. It hosts a range of dance productions, plays, variety and comedy, from contemporary ballet to performances from the Scottish Opera.

➕ F7 ✉ 13–29 Nicolson Street EH8 9FT ☎ 0131 529 6000 🚌 2, 3, 5, 7, 8, 14, 29, 31, 33, 37, 42, 49

ESPIONAGE

espionage007.co.uk

Dance the night away at this popular complex, with its four spy-themed bars and one dance floor.

➕ D6 ✉ 9 Victoria Street EH1 1EX ☎ 0131 477 7007 🕐 Nightly 7pm–3am (to 5am during Festival) 🚌 2, 23, 27, 41

FILMHOUSE

filmhousecinema.com

Opposite the Usher Hall, this art-house cinema has three screens that show the best in art-house and foreign-language cinema from around the globe.

➕ B7 ✉ 88 Lothian Road EH3 9BZ ☎ 0131 228 2688 🚌 10, 11, 15, 17, 16, 34

FRANKENSTEIN PUB

frankensteinedinburgh.co.uk

In a former Pentecostal church, Frankenstein is a bar, restaurant and club themed to bring a chill to the spine. Have a meal, take a drink in one of the three bars or join a themed party, karaoke or games night.

➕ E7 ✉ 26 George IV Bridge EH1 1EN ☎ 0131 622 1818 🕐 Daily noon–1am 🚌 23, 27, 41, 42

THE JAZZ BAR

thejazzbar.co.uk

This intimate, laid-back basement venue serves great cocktails and its musical menu embraces acoustic blues, funk and soul as well as jazz. There are up to five performances daily.

✚ E7 ✉ 1A Chambers Street EH1 1HR
☎ 0131 220 4298 🚌 23, 27, 41, 42, 45

JOLLY JUDGE

jollyjudge.co.uk

One of the first free WiFi hotspots in the city, this characterful 17th-century pub offers a wide choice of malt whiskies. It's difficult to find but worth the search.

✚ D6 ✉ 7 James Court, off Lawnmarket EH1 2PB ☎ 0131 225 2669 🚌 23, 27, 35, 41, 42

KING'S THEATRE

edtheatres.com

One of Edinburgh's oldest theaters is housed in a handsome Edwardian building. A diverse range of shows and musicals, pantomime, comedy, plays and international opera are performed during the Festival.

✚ C8 ✉ 2 Leven Street EH3 9LQ ☎ 0131 529 6000 🚌 11, 15, 16, 17, 23

QUEEN'S HALL

thequeenshall.net

In a converted church, this intimate venue offers a range of events, from jazz and blues to rock and classical music, and comedy from top-class performers. It's home to the Scottish Chamber Orchestra.

✚ F9 ✉ 85–89 Clerk Street EH8 9JG
☎ 0131 668 2019 🚌 3, 5, 7, 8, 29, 31, 37

ROYAL LYCEUM THEATRE

lyceum.org.uk

This magnificent Victorian theater creates all its own shows. Contemporary and classic productions feature, as well as new works.

✚ B7 ✉ Grindlay Street EH3 9AX ☎ 0131 248 4848 (box office) 🚌 1, 10, 11, 15, 16, 17, 22, 34

TRAVERSE THEATRE

traverse.co.uk

This state-of-the-art venue next to the Usher Hall is respected for its experimental plays and dance productions; here you can see hot new work by Scottish playwrights.

✚ B7 ✉ 10 Cambridge Street EH1 2ED
☎ 0131 228 1404 🚌 10, 11, 22

USHER HALL

usherhall.co.uk

Usher Hall is a prestigious concert venue that attracts top performers. The list has included José Carreras, Emeli Sandé, the English Chamber Orchestra and the Moscow Philharmonic.

✚ B7 ✉ Lothian Road EH1 2EA ☎ 0131 228 1155 🚌 1, 10, 11, 15, 16, 17, 22, 34

INTERNATIONAL FILM FESTIVAL

Edinburgh International Film Festival is the longest-running event of its kind in the world, having produced innovative and exciting cinema since 1947. It began with a focus on documentary film, and evolved into a pioneering force for the world of cinema. A celebration of cinema and a showcase for new films from all over the world, it presents UK and world premieres, video shorts and animation. The festival takes place across Edinburgh's cinemas and runs for the last two weeks in June. For information, contact the Edinburgh International Film Festival (✉ 88 Lothian Road EH3 9BZ ☎ 0131 228 4051 or 0131 623 8030; edfilmfest.org.uk).

Where to Eat

PRICES

Prices are approximate, based on a 3-course meal for one person.

£££ over £25
££ £15–£25
£ under £15

AMBER RESTAURANT (££)

amber-restaurant.co.uk

In the Scotch Whisky Experience (▷ 31), Amber offers a lunchtime menu of Scottish cuisine for visitors and shoppers. The ambience is transformed in the evening, with soft velvet drapes enclosing a more intimate space to make a romantic setting for a first-class meal. Menus are seasonal and built around locally sourced ingredients.

🔟 D6 ⊠ 354 Castlehill, The Royal Mile EH1 2NE ☎ 0131 477 8477 ⏰ Sun–Thu 12–8.30, Fri–Sat 12–10 🚌 23, 27, 41, 42

ANGELS WITH BAGPIPES (££)

angelswithbagpipes.co.uk

A sophisticated restaurant that stands out from the run-of-the-mill eating places in this part of town, Angels with Bagpipes serves imaginative Scottish-fusion dishes. The upstairs dining room looks down on Roxburgh Court, and there's a courtyard where you can eat outdoors on sunny days.

🔟 E6 ⊠ 343 High Street EH1 1PW ☎ 0131 222 1111 ⏰ Daily 12–10 🚌 23, 27, 41, 42, 67

BENNETS BAR (£)

Popular with actors from the nearby King's Theatre (▷ 41), this Victorian bar prides itself on sound, simple, home-made food at a good price, and 100 or so malt whiskies. The elaborate interior includes stained glass, tiles, mirrors and carved wood.

🔟 B9 ⊠ 8 Leven Street EH3 9LG ☎ 0131 229 5143 ⏰ Bar meals Mon–Sat 12–2, 5–8.30 🚌 11, 17, 23

DEACON BRODIE'S TAVERN (£)

nicholsonspubs.co.uk

This traditional pub is a popular spot for locals and visitors alike. Bar snacks are served downstairs, while the upstairs restaurant is more formal. Find out more about the infamous Brodie, one of the inspirations for Stevenson's *Dr. Jekyll and Mr. Hyde*, while you sip your pint.

🔟 D6 ⊠ 435 Lawnmarket EH1 2NT ☎ 0131 225 6531 ⏰ Daily 11am–1am 🚌 23, 27, 35, 41, 42

ELEPHANT HOUSE (£)

elephanthouse.biz

Famous for being the place where J.K. Rowling sat down to write the first Harry Potter story, this popular café offers snacks, light meals and tempting cakes.

🔟 E7 ⊠ 21 George IV Bridge EH1 1EN ☎ 0131 220 5355 ⏰ Sun–Thu 8am–10pm, Fri–Sat 8am–11pm 🚌 23, 27, 41, 42

TIPS FOR EATING OUT

Many Edinburgh restaurants can seat customers who walk in off the street, but if you have your heart set on eating at a particular establishment reserve a table in advance. Most restaurants are happy to serve a one- or two-course meal, if that is all you want. If you pay by credit card, when you key in your PIN you may be prompted to leave a tip. It's acceptable to ignore this and leave a cash tip instead. The normal amount, assuming you are happy with the service, is about 10 percent. In Edinburgh it is fairly common for a reservation to last only a couple of hours, after which time you will be expected to vacate the table for the next sitting.

GRAIN STORE (££–£££)

grainstore-restaurant.co.uk

This smart restaurant has a unique setting in an 18th-century stone vaulted storeroom with archways and intimate alcoves. Everything on the well-balanced menu is made in house, from the bread to the desserts. The set-price meals are good value for money.

🔒 D6 ✉ 30 Victoria Street (1st floor) EH1 2JW ☎ 0131 225 7635 🕐 Mon–Sat 12–2.30, 6–9.45, Sun 6–9.30 🚌 2, 23, 27, 41

HANAM'S (££)

hanams.com

This restaurant has several colorful rooms over two floors, plus an open-air terrace for summer dining. The menu is authentically Kurdish, with dishes such as *gormeh sabzi* (Persian-style lamb in spinach) and lamb *tashreeb*, a rich spicy stew. Hanam's does not have an alcohol license, but you can bring your own.

🔒 D6 ✉ 3 Johnston Terrace EH1 2PW ☎ 0131 225 1329 🕐 Daily 12–11 🚌 23, 27, 41, 42, 67

THE MITRE (££)

nicholsonspubs.co.uk

Part of a chain that also includes the legendary Deacon Brodie's further up the Mile, the Mitre serves decent pub food (steak and ale pie, fish and chips, steak and so on) in an attractive old building. There's a good range of real ales and malt whiskies, too.

🔒 F6 ✉ 133 High Street EH1 1SG ☎ 0131 652 3902 🕐 Mon–Thu 12–12, Fri–Sat 12pm–1am 🚌 35

MUMS (££)

monstermashcafe.co.uk

MUMS' subtitle is Great Comfort Food, and the menu is filled with dishes such as sausage and mashed potato, pies

and burgers. The bangers come in many varieties, such as Auld Reekie (smoked) and Mediterranean (with basil and sun-dried tomatoes), and there is a variety of mash to go with them, too. Plastic tomato-shaped ketchup bottles help set the tone.

🔒 E7 ✉ 4a Forrest Road EH1 2QN ☎ 0131 260 9806 🕐 Mon–Sat 9am–10pm, Sun 10–10 🚌 35, 45

OINK (£)

oinkhogroast.co.uk

This popular, no-nonsense café serves great hog rolls, made famous in the Farmers' Market. The hog roast is displayed prominently in the window. You can have your roll with or without crackling (salted crunchy pork rind), and choose your relish. Find a seat if you can, or take out. There is a second establishment at 82 Canongate.

🔒 D6 ✉ 34 Victoria Street EH1 2JW ☎ 07771 968233 🕐 Daily 10am–11pm 🚌 2, 23, 27, 41

ONDINE (£££)

ondinerestaurant.co.uk

Seafood tops the bill at this smart restaurant beneath the stylish Missoni Hotel. The roast shellfish platter is a tasty melange of clams, lobster, mussels and langoustines. Other good fish

---

PUB GRUB

Central-city dining pubs traditionally serve snacks and light meals such as sandwiches, toasted sandwiches, filled potatoes and ploughmans (bread, cheese and pickles). Nowadays, many have extended their menu to include such dishes as curry, steak-and-ale pie, steak and chips or even haggis and neeps (a blend of swede and potato mashed with butter and milk).

dishes include sea bass and John Dory. Service is attentive, and the overall atmosphere is pleasantly unstuffy.

➕ D6 ✉ 2 George IV Bridge EH1 1AD ☎ 0131 226 1888 🕐 Mon–Sat 12–2.30, 5.30–10 🚌 23, 27, 41, 42, 67

ONE SQUARE (££)

onesquareedinburgh.co.uk

This smart, modern bar-restaurant close to the theater district is handy for dinner or drinks before or after a show. The menu features classic British cooking based on fine Scottish ingredients ranging from Black Isle beef to west coast scallops and oysters, Stornoway black pudding and Shetland mussels.

➕ B7 ✉ 1 Festival Square EH3 9SR ☎ 0131 221 6422 🕐 Daily 8pm–1am 🚌 1, 10, 11, 15, 16, 24, 34, 36, 36, 47

PETIT PARIS (££)

petitparis-restaurant.co.uk

France meets Scotland at this friendly country-style bistro. The authentic French cooking features regional specialties—for example from Alsace. The restaurant is a member of Slow Food Scotland.

➕ D7 ✉ 38–40 Grassmarket EH1 2JU ☎ 0131 226 2442 🕐 Sun–Fri 12–3, 5.30–late, Sun 12–late 🚌 2

TOWER RESTAURANT (£££)

tower-restaurant.com

On the fifth floor of the National Museum of Scotland, with great views of the castle, this chic, stylish restaurant offers an interesting selection of eclectic dishes using quality Scottish ingredients, including lobster from the Isle of Skye and venison from Perthshire.

➕ E7 ✉ National Museum of Scotland, Chambers Street EH1 1JF ☎ 0131 225 0973 🕐 Daily 12–11 🚌 2, 23, 27, 35, 41, 42

WHISKI ROOMS (££)

whiskirooms.co.uk

This world-class whisky bar and bistro offers a choice of some 300 single malts and blended whiskies. The menu emphasizes Scottish beef, lamb, steaks and seafood and there are some temptingly sticky puddings.

➕ D6 ✉ 4–7 North Bank Street EH1 2HP ☎ 0131 225 7224 🕐 Daily 12–10 🚌 23, 27, 41, 42, 67

WITCHERY BY THE CASTLE (£££)

thewitchery.com

This enchanting oak-paneled and candlelit restaurant is the place for a special night out. The cooking adds a contemporary twist to Scottish classics like game, fish and seafood, with signature dishes including Angus beef steak tartare and seafood platters. There is a huge selection of wines. The set meals offer the best value.

➕ D6 ✉ Castlehill, Royal Mile EH1 2NF ☎ 0131 225 5613 🕐 Daily 12–11.30 🚌 23, 27, 35, 41, 42

FOOD ON THE RUN

Edinburgh has lots of quick options when you don't want to stop for long. There are food courts in shopping malls, while many attractions have their own restaurants and cafés. American fast-food chains have reached most corners of Scotland, so you won't have to look far to find a pizza or hamburger. The city is liberally sprinkled with very good takeout sandwich bars. Although Edinburgh has many traditional cafés, the word "café" is used to describe the increasing number of more stylish Continental-style establishments, which bridge the gap between pubs, restaurants and coffee bars by selling coffees, snacks, wines and meals.

At the east end of the Royal Mile is the Canongate, culminating in the modern Scottish Parliament Building, the Palace of Holyroodhouse and the open space of Holyrood Park to relax in after sightseeing.

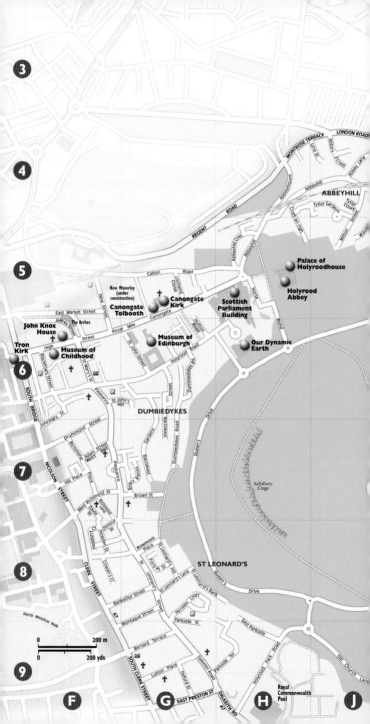

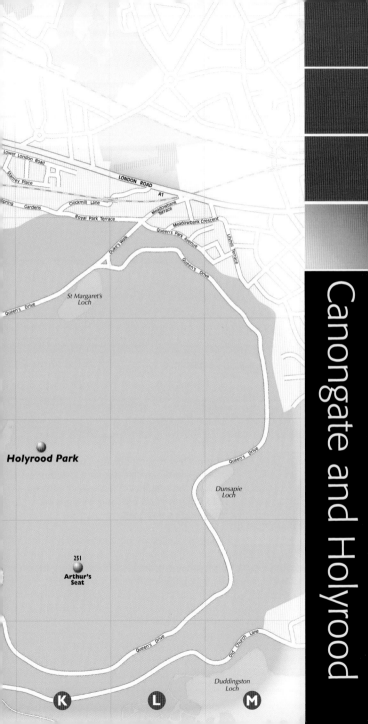

Lower London Road

Stanley Place

Spring Gardens

LONDON ROAD

A1

Clockmill Lane

Royal Park Terrace

Meadowbank Terrace

Meadowbank Crescent

Queen's Park Avenue

Lilyhill Terrace

Duke's Walk

Queen's Drive

Queen's Drive

St Margaret's Loch

Holyrood Park

Queen's Drive

Dunsapie Loch

251

Arthur's Seat

Queen's Drive

Old Church Lane

Duddingston Loch

Canongate and Holyrood

K   L   M

● Spectacular views
● The walk to the top
● Dunsapie Loch and
bird reserve

TIP

● Try to pick a clear day to get the best from the views. It's a waste to make the effort if it's a "dreich" day, as the Scots call a dismal dull day.

The perfect antidote to the stresses of the city, with spectacular views, Arthur's Seat is the remains of an extinct volcano 325 million years old, and it's right on Edinburgh's doorstep.

Geological background The green hill of Arthur's Seat is a city landmark, 251m (823ft) high and visible for miles. Formed during the early Carboniferous era, it is surrounded by seven smaller hills. The summit marks where the cone erupted and molten rock formed the high cliffs of Salisbury Crags. During the Ice Age, erosion exposed the twin peaks of Arthur's Seat and the Crow Hill. There are several explanations for the name; some say it is a corruption of the Gaelic name for archers, others that the Normans associated it with King Arthur.

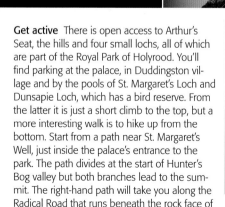

Get active There is open access to Arthur's Seat, the hills and four small lochs, all of which are part of the Royal Park of Holyrood. You'll find parking at the palace, in Duddingston village and by the pools of St. Margaret's Loch and Dunsapie Loch, which has a bird reserve. From the latter it is just a short climb to the top, but a more interesting walk is to hike up from the bottom. Start from a path near St. Margaret's Well, just inside the palace's entrance to the park. The path divides at the start of Hunter's Bog valley but both branches lead to the summit. The right-hand path will take you along the Radical Road that runs beneath the rock face of the Salisbury Crags. The left path goes through Piper's Walk to the top. From here the whole panorama of Edinburgh, the Firth of Forth, the Pentland hills and the coast lies before you.

THE BASICS

✚ K8

✉ Holyrood Park

🎫 Free access, but no vehicular access to the park (except for Dunsapie Loch) on Sun

🚌 35 and then walk through park; or 4, 5, 44, 45 to Meadowbank and walk

♿ Few

Canongate Tolbooth

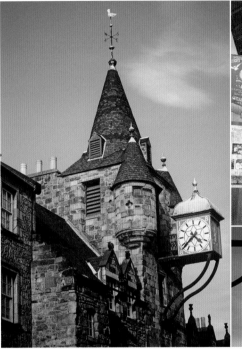

THE PEOPL

HIGHLIGHTS

- The building
- Prison cell
- 1940s kitchen
- Cooper's workshop
- Re-created pub

TIP

- Visit the museum early on in your trip to Edinburgh to give you an insight into the background of the people who made the city what it is today.

Dating from 1591, this French-style Tolbooth has served as both a council chamber and a prison. It now houses the People's Story, a museum of everyday life since the 18th century.

From toll-house to museum The Tolbooth, with its distinctive turreted steeple, is the oldest remaining building in this district and marked the boundary between Holyrood and Edinburgh proper. It served as the council chamber and prison for the independent burgh of Canongate until its incorporation into the city in 1856. The huge boxed clock that projects above the street was added in 1884.

Edinburgh life The building is now home to The People's Story, a museum dedicated to

Clockwise from far left: the turreted Canongate Tolbooth, home to The People's Story museum; trade union banners; passing the time down the pub, one of the museum's displays; the struggle for the right to vote, the people of Edinburgh on the march; all aboard—a clippie model at the museum; the museum sign

everyday life and times in Edinburgh from the 18th century up to the present day. Using oral history, written sources and the reminiscences of local people, it creates a fascinating insight. Indulge your senses through the visual displays, sounds and smells that evoke life in a prison cell, a draper's shop and a cooper's (barrel maker's) workshop. See a servant at work and a tramcar conductor (a clippie, who clipped the tickets). The museum portrays the struggle for improved conditions and people's rights, and explores the role played by the trades union movement and friendly societies, who looked after their members before the welfare state.

Time off Check out the places the locals went to for such leisure time as they had, such as the re-created pub, tearoom and washhouse.

THE BASICS

edinburghmuseums.org.uk

🔁 G5

✉ 163 Canongate EH8 8BN

☎ 0131 529 4057

🕐 Wed–Sat 10–5; also Sun 12–5 in Aug

🚌 35

♿ Good

💷 Free

❓ Shop stocks a wide range of local social history books

Holyrood Park

Arthur's Seat, at the heart of Holyrood Park (left); festival time in the park (right)

THE BASICS

historic-scotland.gov.uk

➕ K7

✉ Holyrood Park

☎ Historic Scotland
Ranger Service: 0131 652
8150

🎟 Free access, but no
vehicular access to the
park (except for Dunsapie
Loch) on Sun

🚌 35 to palace entrance;
other buses to perimeter

♿ Varies; phone for
details

🚻 Free

❓ Leaflets with walking
routes are available from
staff in the hut in Broad
Street car park (by
Holyrood Palace) and from
the Holyrood Lodge
Information Centre (by the
Scottish Parliament), daily
9.30–3.30

HIGHLIGHTS

● Arthur's Seat (▷ 48–49)
● Dunsapie Loch
● St. Margaret's Well

It's a pleasant surprise to discover a city park containing such wild countryside. You'll even find small lochs here.

City's green treasure A royal park since the 12th century, Holyrood Park was enclosed by a stone boundary wall in 1541. Spreading out behind the Palace of Holyroodhouse (▷ 58–59), it extends to some 263ha (650 acres) and is dominated by the great extinct volcano Arthur's Seat (▷ 48–49). It represents a microcosm of Scottish landscape, boasting four lochs, open moorland, marshes, glens and dramatic cliffs, the Salisbury Crags, which inspired Sir Arthur Conan Doyle's novel *The Lost World*.

Get your boots on The park is circled by Queen's Drive, built at the instigation of Prince Albert and closed to commercial vehicles. The area around Dunsapie Loch gives a real sense of remote countryside and is a good spot to start the ascent to Arthur's Seat. It is particularly peaceful here when cars are prohibited on Sunday. All in all, the Park is an excellent place to walk, cycle or picnic.

More to see Also in the park is St. Margaret's Well, a medieval Gothic structure near the palace, where a clear spring wells from beneath sculpted vaulting. Above St. Margaret's Loch, a 19th-century artificial lake, are the remains of St. Anthony's Chapel. On the edge of the park is Duddingston village and the attractive Duddingston Loch.

Fairground rides and puppets on display at the Museum of Childhood

TOP 25

Museum of Childhood

This has been described as "the noisiest museum in the world" and it is popular with both children and adults. Introduce your children to the past and maybe relive it yourself.

Nostalgic pleasure The Museum of Childhood is a delight and claims to be the first museum in the world dedicated to the history of childhood. It was the brainchild of town councillor Joseph Patrick Murray, who argued that the museum was about children rather than for them. Opened in 1955, the collection has grown to display a nostalgic treasure trove of dolls and dolls' houses, train sets and teddy bears. Every aspect of childhood is covered here, from education and medicine to clothing and food. Don't miss the 1930s schoolroom, complete with the chanting of multiplication tables, and watch the street games of Edinburgh children in the 1950s.

Awakening memories There are older items here, such as Victorian dolls and German automata, but probably the best part is recognizing the objects from your own childhood in the collection of playthings from the 1950s to the 90s here, from Scalextric to the Teletubbies.

Founding father Joseph Patrick Murray said that his museum explored a specialized field of social history. From the beginning he put his own mark on the huge array of exhibits, with his slant on informative labels.

THE BASICS

edinburghmuseums.org.uk

➕ F6

✉ 42 High Street, Royal Mile EH1 1TG

☎ 0131 529 4142

🕐 Mon, Thu–Sat 10–5, Sun 12–5

🚌 35 and all North Bridge buses

♿ Very good

🎟 Free

HIGHLIGHTS

● Extensive toy collection
● Re-creation of 1930s classroom
● Victorian dolls
● Dolls' houses
● Automata

TIP

● Check in advance for the schedule of regularly changing exhibitions and varied events to get the most out of your visit.

Museum of Edinburgh

HIGHLIGHTS

● Huntly House building
● Greyfriars Bobby—collar and bowl
● National Covenant
● Earl Haig memorabilia

Edinburgh's own museum is in Huntly House, a 16th-century home much altered in subsequent centuries and at one time occupied by a trade guild.

Picturesque house Just across the road from the Canongate Tolbooth (▷ 50–51), the building housing the Museum of Edinburgh is distinguished by its three pointed gables. Robert Chambers, a Victorian antiquarian, called Huntly House "the speaking house" owing to the Latin inscriptions on the facade.

What's on show The museum is filled with all those local details that bring the history of a city to life. The collections include maps and prints, silver, glass and a vibrant assortment of old shop signs. There is also a fine collection of

From left: models of Highlanders used to advertise tobacconists' shops and other services; re-creation of a room in an 18th-century merchant's house

ceramics and examples of Scottish pottery, as well as items relating to Field Marshal Earl Haig, commander of the British Expeditionary Force in World War I. Of particular interest is the collar and bowl that once belonged to Greyfriars Bobby (▷ 26), together with the original plaster model for the bronze statue of the dog in Candlemaker Row. The family activity area has interactive learning displays to appeal to kids. The museum regularly presents temporary exhibitions that further highlight aspects of local life and are drawn from the extensive local history and decorative arts collections.

Historical Covenant Also on show is the original National Covenant signed by Scotland's Presbyterian leadership in 1638, which is one of the city's greatest treasures.

THE BASICS

edinburghmuseums.org.uk

✚ G6

✉ Huntly House, 142 Canongate, Royal Mile EH8 8DD

☎ 0131 529 4143

🕐 Mon, Thu–Sat 10–5, Sun 12–5

🚌 35

♿ Poor

💷 Free

Our Dynamic Earth

In the jaws of a saber-toothed tiger (left); the Restless Earth exhibit (right)

THE BASICS

dynamicearth.co.uk

⊞ H6

✉ 112 Holyrood Road EH8 8AS

☎ 0131 550 7800

🕐 Apr–Oct daily 10–5.30, (Jul–Aug 10–6); Nov–Mar Wed–Sun 10–5.30

🍴 The Food Chain café

🚌 35

♿ Excellent

💷 Expensive

❓ Well-stocked gift shop—Natural Selection

HIGHLIGHTS

● Striking building
● Time Machine
● Casualties and Survivors gallery
● Tropical Rainforest
● "Submarine trip"
● Restless Earth experience
● FutureDome
● Earthscape Scotland

The tented, spiky roof rising like a white armadillo on the edge of Holyrood Park is Edinburgh's Millennium project: a science park that thrills at every turn.

Popular science This interactive spectacular tells the story of the Earth and its changing nature, from the so-called Big Bang (as viewed from the bridge of a space ship in the How It All Started gallery) to the present day (exactly who lives where in the rainforest).

Stunning effects With 12 galleries devoted to the planet, the underlying message is that the world is a fascinating and ever-changing place. Experience the effect of erupting volcanoes, the icy chill of the polar regions and even a simulated earthquake. You may get caught in a humid rainstorm in the Tropical Rainforest. Every 15 minutes the sky darkens, lightning flashes, thunder roars and torrential rain descends. You can travel in the Time Machine, where stars are created using lights and mirrors. A multiscreen flight over mountains and glaciers is a dizzying highlight. Earthscape Scotland is a trip through geological time and FutureDome is an exciting interactive journey into the future. Casualties and Survivors follows the evolution and adaptation of creatures and plants.

Plenty of stamina Our Dynamic Earth is a popular, impressive feat of high-tech ingenuity. Hardly a relaxing experience, it's exciting to visit, although peak times are likely to be crowded.

Scottish Parliament Building

The Scotland Act in 1998 established the first Scottish Parliament since 1707. It has been at this controversial building since 2004.

Setting the scene From 1999, the Scottish Parliament was housed in buildings around the Royal Mile. Debating took place in the Church of Scotland Assembly at the top of the Mound. The then First Minister Donald Dewar commissioned a new parliament building to be constructed opposite Holyrood Palace, at an original estimated cost of around £40 million. The building was finally opened by the Queen in October 2004, by which time the cost had soared to over £400 million. This expense caused a good deal of controversy, but the resulting building was seen as a success.

No expense spared The innovative and critically acclaimed complex was the work of Barcelona-based architect Enric Miralles. The building is set within landscaped public gardens, against a backdrop of the Salisbury Crags. Inspired by the surrounding scenery, Rennie Mackintosh's flower paintings and upturned boats on the seashore, Miralles wanted to create a building that looked as if it were growing out of the land. The effect is enhanced by copious use of natural materials, with intricate details in oak and sycamore offsetting the granite and smooth concrete finishes. The Debating Chamber, where the 129 members meet, has a striking oak-beamed ceiling.

THE BASICS

visitparliament.scot

✚ H5

✉ The Scottish Parliament, Holyrood Road EH99 1SP

☎ 0131 348 5200

🕐 Business days (Tue–Thu) 9–6.30. Non-business days (Mon, Fri–Sat) and when Parliament is in recess Apr–Sep 10–5 (Tue–Thu 9–6.30); Oct–Mar 10–4

🍴 Café

🚌 35

♿ Excellent

🎫 Free

❓ Guided tours lasting 1 hour are available on most non-business days. Reserve tickets for Public Gallery in advance. Shop sells exclusive items branded to the Scottish Parliament

HIGHLIGHTS

● Architecture
● Exhibition on Scottish Parliament
● Public Gallery

Palace of Holyroodhouse

HIGHLIGHTS

● State apartments
● Queen's Gallery
● Chambers of Mary, Queen of Scots

TIP

● It is best to phone ahead as the palace is closed to visitors whenever a member of the royal family is in residence and security surrounding the building is extremely tight.

Founded as a monastery in 1128, today the palace is the Queen's official residence in Scotland. The pepperpot-towered castle is set against the backdrop of majestic Arthur's Seat, at the foot of the Royal Mile.

Steeped in royal history In the 15th century the palace became a guest house for the nearby Holyrood Abbey (now a scenic ruin), and its name is said to derive from the Holy Rood, a fragment of Christ's Cross belonging to King David I (c. 1080–1153). Mary, Queen of Scots stayed here, and a brass plate marks where her Italian favorite, David Rizzio, was murdered in her private apartments in the west tower in 1566. During the Civil War in 1650 the palace was seriously damaged and major

Clockwise from far left: crowning glory—a royal lantern outside the Palace of Holyroodhouse; a stone unicorn stands guard; the mellow evening light enhances the fairy-tale palace; lion detail on the gates; a view of the palace and Arthur's Seat from Calton Hill

rebuilding was necessary. Bonnie Prince Charlie held court here in 1745, followed by George IV on his triumphant visit to the city in 1822, and later by Queen Victoria en route to Balmoral.

Home and art gallery The palace offers all the advantages of exploring a living space steeped in history and filled with works of art from the Royal Collection. More precious artworks are on view in the stunning Queen's Gallery, by the entrance and opposite the new Scottish Parliament. The state rooms, designed by architect William Bruce (1630–1710) for Charles II and hung with Brussels tapestries, are particularly elaborate and ornately splendid. Don't miss the 110 preposterous royal portraits painted in a hurry by Jacob de Wet in 1684–86, which are hung in the Great Gallery.

THE BASICS

royalcollection.org.uk

✛ H5

✉ Canongate, Royal Mile EH8 8DX

☎ 0131 556 5100

🕓 Apr–Oct daily 9.30–6; Nov–Mar daily 9.30–4.30. May close at short notice

🍴 In old coach house

🚌 35, 36

♿ Good

💷 Expensive

❓ Free audio tour available. Gift shop stocks cards, books and china

More to See

CANONGATE KIRK

canongatekirk.org.uk

Built in 1688, this church's distinctive Dutch gable and plain interior reflect the Canongate's trading links with the Low Countries. Note the gilded stag's head at the gable top, traditionally a gift of the monarch. Buried in the graveyard are economist and philosopher Adam Smith (1723–90) and David Rizzio, darling of Mary, Queen of Scots, murdered in 1566.

➕ G5 ✉ Canongate EH8 8BR ☎ 0131 556 3515 🕐 Jun–Sep Mon–Sat 10.30–4, Sun service at 11.15; burial ground open all year 🚌 35 ♿ Good 💷 Free (donations welcomed)

HOLYROOD ABBEY

Founded by King David I in 1128, the present structure was built in the early 13th century. With the reformation the church gradually fell into decline, and it was finally abandoned in 1768 when the roof caved in. You can only see the ruins on a visit to the Palace (▷ 58–59).

JOHN KNOX HOUSE

tracscotland.org

Dating to the 15th century, the house is typical of the period, with overhanging gables and picturesque windows. Inside is a museum with displays relating to Knox and to James Mosman, jeweler to Mary, Queen of Scots. The house is also home to the Scottish Storytelling Centre (▷ 64).

➕ F6 ✉ 43–45 High Street EH1 1SR ☎ 0131 556 9579 🕐 Mon–Sat 10–6, Sun (Jul–Aug only) 12–6 🚌 35 and all North Bridge buses ♿ Ground floor only 💷 Inexpensive

TRON KIRK

This fine early Scottish Renaissance church derives its name from the salt-tron, a public weighbeam that once stood outside. The church was deconsecrated in 1952, and is now home to an indoor Victorian market. It is occasionally used as a venue during the Fringe festival.

➕ E6 ✉ High Street EH1 2NG 🚌 35 and all North Bridge buses

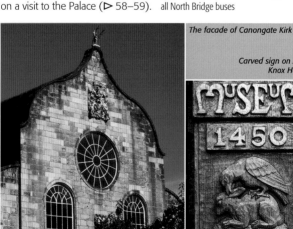

The facade of Canongate Kirk

Carved sign on John Knox House

Through Canongate to Holyrood Park

Walk along High Street to Canongate, with its historic buildings and museums, and then take a break in the glorious Holyrood Park.

DISTANCE: 1.5km (1 mile) **ALLOW:** 1 hour (plus time in the park)

START

TRON KIRK
⊞ E6 🚌 35 and all North Bridge buses

1 Start at the Tron Kirk (▷ 60) on High Street at the junction with South Bridge. Leaving the church to your right, walk up High Street.

2 On your left is the Brass Rubbing Centre, next to which is John Knox House (▷ 60) and opposite the Museum of Childhood (▷ 53). Continue on into Canongate.

3 After about 400m you will come to the Museum of Edinburgh (▷ 54–55) on your right, which gives an excellent insight into the history of the city.

4 On the left, a short distance on, is the old Canongate Tolbooth (▷ 50–51), which houses The People's Story, giving more background to life in historic Edinburgh.

END

HOLYROOD PARK
⊞ K7 🚌 35

8 There are some 263ha (650 acres) to explore here, as well as Our Dynamic Earth (▷ 56) science park and Arthur's Seat (▷ 48–49).

7 Opposite the Parliament, at the end of Canongate (also the end of the Royal Mile), is the Palace of Holyroodhouse (▷ 58–59), with its fine collection of art and royal objects. Behind the palace is the huge expanse of the delightful Holyrood Park (▷ 52).

6 Continue toward the end of Canongate and you will see the Scottish Parliament Building (▷ 57) on the right, deemed an architectural masterpiece by some but an extravagance by others.

5 Just beyond is Canongate Kirk (▷ 60), the striking Dutch-style church.

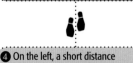

Shopping

CARSON CLARK

carsonclarkgallery.co.uk

This wonderful gallery specializes in antique maps and sea charts from all over the globe, dating from the 16th to 19th centuries, plus replica maps and reproduction prints.

🔲 F6 ✉ 17–21 St. Mary's Street EH1 1TA
☎ 0131 556 4710 🚌 35

CRANACHAN & CROWDIE

cranachanandcrowdie.com

The perfect place to pick up a few presents to take home, this tempting emporium is piled high with Scottish delicacies, from whisky to shortbread.

🔲 F6 ✉ 263 Canongate EH8 8BQ ☎ 0131 556 7194 🚌 35

FUDGE KITCHEN

fudgekitchen.co.uk

This shop offers 20 different varieties of delectable fudge, all handcrafted using traditional methods and the finest ingredients from a recipe dating from 1830.

🔲 F6 ✉ 30 High Street EH1 1TB ☎ 0131 558 1517 🚌 35 and all North Bridge buses

GEOFFREY (TAILOR) KILTMAKERS

geoffreykilts.co.uk

This family-run business produces traditional, casual and modern kilts and related items for men and women,

---

BAGPIPES

The bagpipes are synonymous with Scotland. You see them everywhere, from the Military Tattoo in Edinburgh to school sports days and agricultural shows. There are many types, played in countries all over the world but often associated with the military. Surprisingly, the bagpipes' origins are not even Scottish but possibly ancient Egyptian or Greek.

---

either off the peg or made to measure. You can even design your own tartan. All items are made from high-quality materials in Scotland.

🔲 F6 ✉ 57–59 High Street EH1 1SR
☎ 0131 557 0256 🚌 35 and all North Bridge buses

NEANIE SCOTT

Unlike many of the Royal Mile giftshops, Neanie Scott's range of souvenirs, crafts and weapons is mainly made in Scotland. The friendly proprietor is always ready to chat to visitors and offer advice on purchases.

🔲 G5 ✉ 131 Canongate EH8 8BP ☎ 0131 558 3528 🚌 35

PALENQUE

palenquejewellery.co.uk

Palenque specializes in competitively priced, high-quality contemporary silver rings, necklaces, pendants and bracelets and hand-crafted accessories.

🔲 F6 ✉ 56 High Street EH1 1TB ☎ 0131 557 9553 🚌 35 and all North Bridge buses

RAGAMUFFIN

Displays of vivid handmade chunky knitwear, scarves, accessories and toys catch your eye in the huge windows of this stylish boutique on the corner of St. Mary's Street.

🔲 F6 ✉ 278 Canongate EH8 8AA ☎ 0131 557 6007 🚌 35

WILLIAM CADENHEAD

wmcadenhead.com

This quaint shop, hidden at the bottom of the Royal Mile, advertises itself as Scotland's oldest independent bottler and specializes in malt whiskies and old oak-matured Demerara rum.

🔲 G6 ✉ 172 Canongate EH8 8BN ☎ 0131 556 5864 🚌 35

Entertainment and Nightlife

BONGO CLUB

thebongoclub.co.uk

By day an arts center, café and exhibition space, Bongo transforms at night into a venue for live music, drama and the club scene.

🔝 E7 ✉ 66 Cowgate EH1 1JX ☎ 0131 558 8844 🕐 Daily 10pm–3am (but times can vary) 🚌 35 and all South Bridge buses

SCOTTISH STORYTELLING CENTRE

tracscotland.org

This venue stages Scottish and children's plays, and story and poetry readings.

🔝 F6 ✉ 43–45 High Street EH1 1SR ☎ 0131 556 9579 🕐 Mon–Sat 10–6, Sun (Jul–Aug only) 12–6 🚌 35 and all North Bridge buses 🚻 Good 🎫 Some events free

WAVERLEY BAR

The walls and ceiling of this tiny, quirky, old-fashioned bar are plastered with posters from long-forgotten bands and Fringe performances. It still hosts live music and (on the last Friday of each month) storytelling events.

🔝 F6 ✉ 1 St. Mary's Street EH1 1TA ☎ 0131 557 1050 🕐 Daily 7pm–11pm (sometimes later during Festival) 🚌 35 🎫 Free

WHISTLEBINKIES

whistlebinkies.com

This local favorite offers live music (mainly rock and folk) every night.

🔝 F6 ✉ 4–6 South Bridge EH1 1LL ☎ 0131 557 5114 🕐 Daily 5pm–3am (exact performance times vary) 🚌 23, 24, 27, 29, 41, 42, 45 🎫 Free

Where to Eat

PRICES
Prices are approximate, based on a 3-course meal for one person.
£££   over £25
££   £15–£25
£   under £15

THE CANONS' GAIT (££)

gait.bar

This lively gastropub offers a good selection of Scottish real ales and an imaginative menu, which specializes in meaty dishes such as sausage and mash, venison or pig's cheek and pig's ear.

🔝 F6 ✉ 232 Canongate EH8 8DQ ☎ 0131 556 4481 🕐 Meals Mon–Sat 12–8; bar Mon–Thu 12–11, Fri–Sat 12pm–1am 🚌 35

DAVID BANN

davidbann.co.uk

David Bann's well-designed restaurant makes good use of natural wood and soft lighting to set the mood for modern vegan and vegetarian cuisine.

✉ F6 ✉ 56–58 St. Mary's Street EH1 1SX ☎ 0131 556 5888 🕐 Mon–Fri 12–10, Sat–Sun 11–10

DUBH PRAIS RESTAURANT (££)

dubhpraisrestaurant.com

Seek out this romantic cellar restaurant for Scottish far such as haggis, beef, lamb, venison and salmon, garnished with herbs from the chef's garden.

🔝 F6 ✉ 123b High Street EH1 1SG ☎ 0131 557 5732 🕐 Tue–Sat 5–10.30 🚌 23, 27, 35, 41, 42, 45

New Town

The New Town displays Edinburgh's elegant face. The broad Georgian streets are lined with gracious houses with large windows and attractive doorways. Here, too, are the best shopping and eating opportunities.

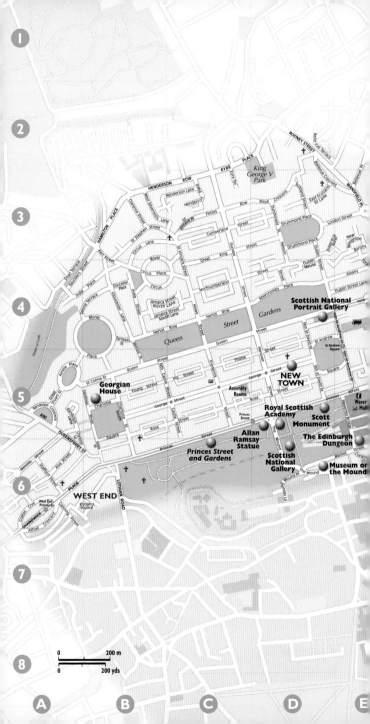

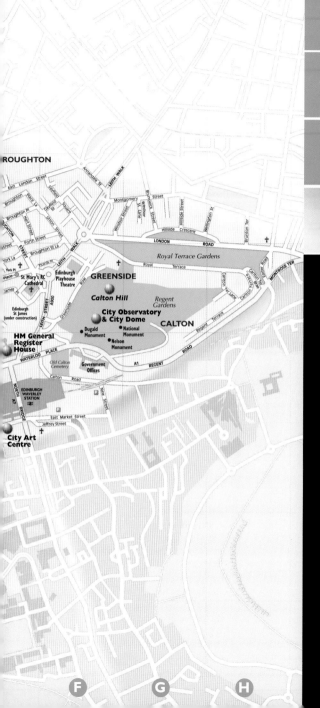

ROUGHTON

East London Street

Annandale St

LEITH WALK

Montgomery Street

Brunswick Street

Broughton Place La

Gayfield Square

Hart Street

Albany Street

Forth Street

Hillside Street

Wellington St

Brunton Ter

Union Street

Broughton St La

Hillside Crescent

York La

Picardy Pl

Leopold Pl

York Pl

LONDON ROAD

St Mary's RC
Cathedral

Edinburgh
Playhouse
Theatre

Royal Terrace Gardens

Royal Terrace

Carlton Ter La

Montrose Ter

James

LEITH STREET

A900

GREENSIDE

Greenside

Calton Hill

Regent
Gardens

Carlton Ter Brae

Carlton Terrace

Regent Road Easter Road

Edinburgh
St James
(under construction)

City Observatory
& City Dome

CALTON

HM General
Register
House

WATERLOO PLACE

Dugald
Monument

National
Monument

Nelson
Monument

NORTH A7 BRIDGE

Old Calton
Cemetery

Government
Offices

A1 REGENT ROAD

Regent Terrace

Calton Road

EDINBURGH
WAVERLEY
STATION

New Street

East Market Street

Jeffrey Street

City Art
Centre

F G H

Calton Hill

TOP
25

The remarkable
Classical buildings of
Calton Hill

THE BASICS

edinburghmuseums.org.uk

🔲 F4

🚌 X26

ℹ️ Edinburgh Museums
and Galleries

☎ 0131 556 2716

HIGHLIGHTS

- Spectacular views
- Nelson Monument
- National Monument
- City Observatory
- Playfair Monument
- Dugald Steward
Monument

Remarkable buildings grace the top of this volcanic hill, and it is also worth the climb for superb views over the city— Robert Louis Stevenson's most-loved vista of Edinburgh.

Grandiose style Calton Hill (108m/354ft) is crowned by the columns of one of Edinburgh's more eccentric edifices. In 1822 work began on the National Monument of Scotland. Inspired by the Parthenon in Athens and built by public subscription, it was to be a monument to Scottish sailors and soldiers killed in the Napoleonic Wars, but in 1829—with only 12 columns completed—the money ran out. The prolific Edinburgh architect William Playfair's grandiose monument became known as "Edinburgh's Disgrace." The remaining folly, however, is part of the distinctive skyline of Calton Hill.

Other monuments Sharing the slopes of Calton Hill with the National Monument are the City Observatory (designed by James Craig) and the Dugald Steward Monument, commemorating the well-known philosopher, another design by William Playfair. Also on the hill is the 1816 tower of the Nelson Monument, a 143-step climb, but worth the effort. The climb to the park at the top is rewarded by superb views. Here on the grassy slopes you can see south to the red-toned cliffs of Salisbury Crags and down to the undulating slopes of Holyrood Park or to the east beyond Princes Street.

Robert Adam's Georgian House (right) has some classic 18th-century displays (left)

Georgian House

This elegant house, with its preserved period interiors, gives you a fascinating glimpse into the lives of the prosperous classes who lived in the New Town in the 18th century.

How the other half lived The north side of Charlotte Square is the epitome of 18th-century New Town elegance and was designed by architect Robert Adam (1728–92) as a single, palace-fronted block. With its symmetrical stonework, rusticated base and ornamented upper levels, it is an outstanding example of the style. The Georgian House, a preserved residence on the north side of the square, oozes gracious living. It is a meticulous re-creation by the National Trust for Scotland, reflecting all the fashionable details of the day, right down to the Wedgwood dinner service on the dining table and the magnificent drawing room with its beautiful candlesticks.

Georgian elegance As you step in the door of this house you can't help but be impressed by the balustraded staircase and its stunning cupola above, flooding the building with light. The stairs lead to the first floor and the Grand Drawing Room, perfect for entertaining.

Below stairs For a contrast, take a look in the basement at the kitchen and the well-scrubbed areas, including the wine cellar and china closet. Here the hard work took place, reflecting the marked social divides of the time.

THE BASICS

nts.org.uk
+ B5
✉ 7 Charlotte Square EH2 4DR
☎ 0131 226 3318
🕐 Jul–Aug daily 10–6; Apr–Jun, Sep–Oct daily 10–5; Mar daily 10–4; Nov daily 11–3
🚌 10, 19, 33, 41 and tram
♿ Limited; six steps to ground floor
💷 Moderate

HIGHLIGHTS

● Staircase and cupola
● Grand Drawing Room
● Dining Room
● Basement with kitchen

HIGHLIGHTS

- Charlotte Square
- The Georgian House
  (▷ 69)
- The Mound

A product of the lack of space in Edinburgh's Old Town, this spectacular piece of Georgian town planning was instigated by a competition in 1766 to build a fine "New Town."

Georgian streets Edinburgh's so-called New Town covers an area of about 318ha (1sq mile) to the north of Princes Street, and is characterized by broad streets of spacious terraced houses with large windows and ornamental door arches. The original area comprised three residential boulevards to run parallel with the Old Town ridge: Princes Street, George Street and Queen Street. With a square at each end (St. Andrew and Charlotte), they were also linked by smaller roads—Rose Street and Thistle Street—to shops and businesses. While Princes

Clockwise from far left: the entrance to this 18th-century house in New Town looks a picture with its floral display; townhouse rooftop detail; typical Georgian fanlight and porch, and ornate lamp outside; created from a huge pile of rubble, the Mound went on to support Edinburgh's most prestigious art galleries

Street has been taken over by commercial activity, wide Charlotte Square, with its pre-served Georgian House (▷ 69), is the epitome of the planners' intentions.

Other highlights It took 2 million cartloads of rubble to create the Mound, later home to the Scottish National Gallery (▷ 72–73) and the Royal Scottish Academy (▷ 76). The Mound came about by accident when clothier "Geordie" Boyd started to dump rubble in the marsh, quickly followed by the builders from the New Town. Farther out is Stockbridge, a former mining village developed as part of a second New Town. It was on land owned by the painter Sir Henry Raeburn and became a bohemian artisans' corner. Ann Street is now one of the city's top addresses (▷ 99).

THE BASICS

➕ D5
ℹ️ Edinburgh and Scotland Information Centre, 3 Princes Street EH2 2QP
☎ 0131 473 3868

Scottish National Gallery

HIGHLIGHTS

● *The Revd Dr Robert Walker Skating on Duddingston Loch* by Sir Henry Raeburn
● Monet's *Haystacks*
● Botticelli's *The Virgin Adoring the Sleeping Christ Child*
● Land- and seascapes by William McTaggart
● Works by Old Masters, including Vermeer, Raphael and Titian

This striking 19th-century building houses superb Old Masters and an outstanding Scottish collection. It is the perfect setting for Scotland's finest art.

Artistic venue The gallery was designed by New Town architect William Playfair (1789–1857) and completed in the year of his death. It is easily spotted thanks to the huge golden stone pillars of its neoclassical flanks and should not be confused with the nearby Royal Scottish Academy, which has been refurbished as an international exhibition venue (▷ 76).

What's on show The gallery's impressive collection of paintings, sculptures and drawings includes more than 20,000 items, displayed in intimate and accessible surroundings. The time

Clockwise from far left: Botticelli's Virgin Adoring the Sleeping Christ Child, *c.1490; busts adorn the gallery stairs; Lorenzo Bartolini's graceful sculpture* The Campbell Sisters *(1821) in front of Benjamin West's* Fury of the Stag, *1786; Monet's* Haystacks: Snow Effect, *1891; Raeburn's* The Revd Dr Robert Walker Skating on Duddingston Loch, *c.1795; the grandiose facade of the gallery*

span runs from the early Renaissance to the end of the 19th century. At the collection's heart are paintings by the great masters of Europe, including Vermeer, Van Gogh, Raphael and Titian. Look out for Monet's *Haystacks* (1891), Velázquez's *Old Woman Cooking Eggs* (1618) and Botticelli's masterpiece *Virgin Adoring the Sleeping Christ Child* (*c.*1490).

Scottish contingent Not surprisingly, the gallery has an outstanding collection of works by Scottish artists. Favorites here include Raeburn's 1795 portrait of *The Revd Dr Robert Walker Skating on Duddingston Loch,* and the sweeping land- and seascapes of William McTaggart. Look out for the vivid scenes of everyday life among the common people, as captured on canvas by Sir David Wilkie.

THE BASICS

nationalgalleries.org

➕ D6

✉ The Mound EH2 2EL

☎ 0131 624 6200

🕐 Daily 10–5, Thu until 7pm

🍴 Café

🚌 3, 10, 17, 23, 24, 27, 44 and others, and tram; a free bus links the National Gallery with the Gallery of Modern Art

♿ Very good

🎟 Free

❓ Shop stocks cards, books and gifts

Princes Street and Gardens

TOP 25

Edinburgh's most famous street at dusk (left); Ross fountain in the gardens (right)

THE BASICS

➕ C6
✉ Princes Street
🕐 Gardens: summer 7am–10pm; winter 7–5
🎟 Free

HIGHLIGHTS

● Great views to the castle
● Jenners department store—the world's oldest (▷ 79)
● Floral clock
● Summer band concerts

Originally designed as a residential area, the most famous street in Scotland is now where local people come to shop. The gardens are a welcome escape from the urban buzz.

Changes over time If you stroll along Queen Street, you can see how it echoes Princes Street and gives an insight into James Craig's original residential plan. He designated today's Thistle and Rose streets, lesser byways between the grand thoroughfares, as the living and business place of tradespeople and shopkeepers. The use of the lanes behind Thistle and Rose streets to reach the back doors of the wealthier residents was a clever element in his scheme. By the mid-19th century developments began to encroach, however, and the gracious Georgian buildings started to deteriorate, some replaced by more utilitarian edifices in the 20th century.

Getting its name Princes Street was originally to be called St. Giles Street, but King George III objected as it reminded him of the St. Giles district of London, which was notorious for its lowlife. The street instead became Princes Street after his two eldest sons.

Oasis of green Princes Street Gardens are a pleasant place to sit down and admire the backs of the Old Town tenements across the valley. In summer there are concerts to enjoy and, an Edinburgh institution since 1902, the floral clock—a flowerbed planted up as a clock.

More to See

ALLAN RAMSAY STATUE

In West Princes Street Gardens is a statue of the former wig-maker turned poet Allan Ramsay (1684–1758), by Sir John Steel (1865).

🔲 D5 ✉ West Princes Street Gardens 🚌 3, 10, 17, 24, 27, 34

CITY ART CENTRE

edinburghmuseums.org.uk

The gallery is housed in a six-floor former warehouse. It stages changing exhibitions and displays the city's collection of Scottish paintings, including works by the 20th-century Scottish Colourists.

🔲 E6 ✉ 2 Market Street EH1 1DE ☎ 0131 529 3993 🕐 Wed–Sat 10–5, Sun 12–5 🍽 Café 🚌 3, 3A, 31, 33, 36 ♿ Very good 🎫 Free; charge for some exhibitions

CITY OBSERVATORY AND CITY DOME

collectivegallery.net

The old City Observatory atop Calton Hill reopened in 2017 and is now fully open to the public for the first time in its history, housing a restaurant and visual arts space. The observatory complex also comprises the City Dome, a venue for art exhibitions.

🔲 F4 ✉ 38 Calton Hill EH7 5AA ☎ 0131 556 1264 🕐 Aug daily 10–6; Apr–Jul, Sep Tue–Sun 10–5; Oct–Mar Tue–Sun 10–4; café daily 10–4 🚌 X26 ♿ Good 🎫 Free

THE EDINBURGH DUNGEON

thedungeons.com

Beneath the paving stones of the city encounter witch-hunters, grave-robbers and murderers. It's not recommended for the fainthearted or very young children.

🔲 E6 ✉ 31 Market Street EH1 1QB ☎ 0131 240 1000 🕐 Jul–Aug daily 10–7; mid-Mar to Jun, Sep–Oct daily 10–5; Nov to mid-Mar Mon–Fri 11–4, Sat–Sun 10.30–4.30 🚌 All buses to Waverley Station (one-minute walk) ♿ Phone for details 🎫 Expensive

HM GENERAL REGISTER HOUSE

nas.gov.uk

Register House was originally sited in the castle, then in the Tolbooth. In 1774 a custom-built Register

The City Observatory complex

House was built in Princes Street to house the national archives. It is guarded by a famous statue of Wellington.

🔲 E5 ✉ Scottish Record Office, 2 Princes Street EH1 3YT ☎ 0131 535 1314 🕐 Mon–Fri 9–4.30 ♿ Good 🚌 Free with reader's ticket; proof of identity required

MUSEUM ON THE MOUND

museumonthemound.com

Located in the bank's headquarters, this small, unusual museum displays old maps, gold coins, bank notes, forgeries and bullion chests.

🔲 D6 ✉ Bank of Scotland Head Office, The Mound EH1 1YZ ☎ 0131 243 5464 🕐 Tue–Fri 10–5, Sat–Sun 1–5 🚌 23, 27, 41, 42 ♿ Good 🚌 Free

ROYAL SCOTTISH ACADEMY

royalscottishacademy.org

William Playfair's lovely Classical building is now linked to the National Gallery to create a superb space for displaying art.

🔲 D5 ✉ The Mound EH2 2EL ☎ 0131 225 6671 🕐 Mon–Sat 10–5, Sun 12–5

🚌 3, 10, 17, 23, 24, 27, 44; free bus links main galleries ♿ Very good 🚌 Free; charge for some exhibitions

SCOTT MONUMENT

edinburghmuseums.org.uk

Generations have climbed this 61m (200ft) structure since it opened in 1846 to appreciate fine views of the city. The stone figures are characters from Sir Walter Scott's novels.

🔲 D5 ✉ East Princes Street Gardens EH2 2EJ ☎ 0131 529 4068 🕐 Apr–Sep daily 10–7; Oct–Mar daily 10–4 (last admission 3.30) 🚌 Moderate

SCOTTISH NATIONAL PORTRAIT GALLERY

nationalgalleries.org

This gallery tells the history of Scotland through the portraits of the great, the good, the bad and the vain: a host of familiar faces.

🔲 D4 ✉ 1 Queen Street EH2 1JD ☎ 0131 624 6200 🕐 Daily 10–5, Thu until 7 🚌 4, 8, 10, 12, 16, 26, 44; free bus links main galleries ♿ Very good 🚌 Free; charge for some exhibitions

View from the Scott Monument

Home to the illustrious, the Scottish National Portrait Gallery

Georgian Facades
of New Town

Explore New Town's streets and squares, full of superb Georgian architecture. For shopping try George Street and Multrees Walk.

DISTANCE: 4km (2.5 miles) **ALLOW:** 1 hour 30 minutes, plus stops

START ·······

PRINCES STREET
🚇 D5 🚌 3, 10, 17, 25, 44

① Start on Princes Street (▷ 74) by the Royal Scottish Academy (▷ 76). Cross over into Hanover Street. Take the second turning on your left and walk along George Street.

② At the end is Charlotte Square, one of the finest examples of Georgian architecture in the city. Turn right and right again into Young Street. At the end turn left and go down North Castle Street.

③ When you reach Queen Street cross over and turn left, then take the next right down Wemyss Place. Turn right into Heriot Row.

④ Here you will find the home of Robert Louis Stevenson. When you reach Howe Street turn left and take the second left into South East Circus Place.

········ **END**

PRINCES STREET
🚇 D5 🚌 3, 10, 17, 25, 44

⑧ In front of you is St. Andrew Square. Go around the square, turning left into North St. David Street, which leads back to Princes Street.

⑦ At the roundabout turn right and walk up Broughton Street, with its good choice of refreshment stops. At the end of the street turn right onto York Place and then turn left onto Elder Street. Take the next right down Multrees Walk (▷ 79, panel).

⑥ At the end turn right onto St. Vincent Street. Cross over into Great King Street and at the end turn right and then immediately left onto Drummond Place and continue ahead into London Street.

⑤ Pause to admire the sweep of the Royal Circus before you bear right for North East Circus Place.

Shopping

EDINBURGH ROCK

ANTHONY WOODD GALLERY

anthonywoodd.com

Traditional art—mainly 19th-century oils, watercolors and prints, from landscapes to sporting and military subjects—is the focus here.

➕ C4 ✉ 4 Dundas Street EH3 6HZ ☎ 0131 558 9544/5 🚌 13, 23, 27

BELINDA ROBERTSON

belindarobertson.com

Scotland's renowned cashmere designer has come to the heart of Edinburgh's New Town. Belinda's creations, which include sweaters, gloves and scarves as well as cashmere knickers and G-strings, have been donned by the likes of Nicole Kidman and Madonna.

➕ C4 ✉ 13A Dundas Street EH3 6QG ☎ 0131 557 8118 🚌 13, 23, 27

THE BROTIQUE

thebrotique.co.uk

This emporium provides stylish menswear, accessories and grooming potions for bearded hipsters and young fogeys.

➕ C5 ✉ 39 Queen Street EH2 3NH ☎ 0131 629 1303 🚌 12, 19, 36, 37, 41, 43

CONCRETE WARDROBE

concretewardrobe.com

This store specializes in clothes, accessories and crafts by local designers such as Blue Marmalade, Pickone, Tessuti and Roobedo, and 20th-century collectibles from the 1920s to the 70s.

➕ E3 ✉ 50A Broughton Street EH1 3SA ☎ 0131 558 7130 🚌 8, 9

CURIOUSER AND CURIOUSER

curiouserandcuriouser.com

Curiouser and Curiouser sells attractive prints and paintings by Scottish artists, illustrated books, pottery, jewelry and colorful cards, toys and accessories.

➕ E3 ✉ 93 Broughton Street EH1 3RZ ☎ 0131 556 1866 🚌 8, 9

HAMILTON & INCHES

hamiltonandinches.com

Established in 1866, the city's most reputable jeweler offers imaginative jewelry and silverware in a grand old building with workshops above and an ornate interior, complete with chandeliers.

➕ C5 ✉ 87 George Street EH2 3EY ☎ 0131 225 4898 🚌 13, 23, 24, 27, 29, 42

HARVEY NICHOLS

harveynichols.com

Scotland's first branch of this exclusive London department store added a touch of glamor when it opened in Edinburgh in 2002; perfumes, designer handbags, accessories and clothes, including Gucci, Burberry, Prada, Fendi and Dior. A bar, brasserie and top-floor restaurant add plenty of options for refreshment after hectic shopping.

➕ E4 ✉ 30–34 St. Andrew Square EH2 2AD ☎ 0131 524 8388 🚌 8, 10, 11, 12, 16

HECTOR RUSSELL

hector-russell.com

Part of a well-known chain of kilt shops, this branch allows you to rent as well as buy. It's all here, from a *sgian dubh* (small knife worn inside the sock) to the complete outfit. The shop will arrange for your purchases to be mailed home. There's another branch in High Street.

➕ C5 ✉ 95 Princes Street EH2 2ER ☎ 0131 220 2493; freephone order number (UK only) 0800 980 4010 🚌 3, 10, 17, 25, 44

JANE DAVIDSON

janedavidson.co.uk

Jane's daughter Sarah has built her reputation on providing excellent service. The three-floor Georgian town house

stocks exclusive cashmere labels from around the world and features many top designers, such as Allegra Hicks and Diane Von Furstenberg.

➕ C5 ✉ 52 Thistle Street EH2 1EN ☎ 0131 225 3280 🚌 23, 27, 29, 42

JENNERS
houseoffraser.co.uk
Edinburgh's grand old dame was founded in 1838 and is now owned by House of Fraser. The magnificent building is a rabbit warren inside, with a central galleried arcade, and houses over 100 departments, from clothes and shoes to perfume, glassware, groceries and toys. There are four cafés.

➕ D5 ✉ 48 Princes Street EH2 2YJ ☎ 0344 800 3725 🚌 3, 10, 17, 23, 24, 27, 44 and others

JOSEPH BONNAR
josephbonnar.com
In business since the 1960s, Joseph Bonnar boasts Scotland's largest range of antique jewelry, plus other items.

➕ C5 ✉ 72 Thistle Street EH2 1EN ☎ 0131 226 2811 🚌 23, 27, 29, 42

LINZI CRAWFORD
linzicrawford.com
The only stockist of several edgy European labels, Linzi also has her own line of merino and cashmere clothing in distinct shades.

➕ D4 ✉ 27 Dublin Street EH3 6NL ☎ 0131 558 7558 🚌 13

MCNAUGHTAN'S BOOKSHOP
mcnaughtansbookshop.com
A highly respected secondhand and antiquarian bookshop where casual browsing can sometimes unearth a real gem. The helpful owner, Elizabeth Strong, will search for specific titles.

➕ F3 ✉ 3a/4a Haddington Place, Leith Walk EH7 4AE ☎ 0131 556 5897 🚌 7, 10, 11, 12, 14, 16, 22, 25, 34, 49

MOLTON BROWN
moltonbrown.co.uk
The simple clean lines of this store are reflected in the products: pampering lotions and delectable fragrances for men and women.

➕ D5 ✉ 35a George Street EH2 2HN ☎ 0131 225 8452 🚌 13, 19, 37, 41

OPEN EYE GALLERY
openeyegallery.co.uk
This small gallery sells the work of Scottish painters, printmakers and sculptors past and present, as well as works by international masters from Picasso to Hockney.

➕ D4 ✉ 34 Abercromby Place EH3 6QE ☎ 0131 558 9872 🚌 19A, 24, 29, 42

PAPER TIGER
papertiger.co.uk
Popular shop selling an attractive range of fun and funky gifts, furnishings and household items.

➕ A6 ✉ 6A–B Stafford Street EH3 7AU ☎ 0131 226 2390 🚌 12, 25, 44

WALK THE WALK
Multrees Walk is a great place for designer shopping in Edinburgh (the-walk.co.uk). The stylish pedestrianized shopping street has attracted a whole host of prestigious international retailers, such as Links of London, Mulberry, Azendi, Calvin Klein, Louis Vuitton, Emporio Armani and Boss. It also boasts a five-floor Harvey Nichols department store (▷ 78), several stylish accessory shops and galleries, and the excellent Valvona & Crolla Vincaffè bar and restaurant (▷ 86).

NEW TOWN SHOPPING

RANDOLPH GALLERY

randolphgallery.com

A small space with changing exhibitions, Randolph deals mainly in realist art from local artists. Dundas Street is the city's main street for contemporary art.

➕ C3 ✉ 39 Dundas Street EH3 6QQ

☎ 0131 556 0808 🚌 13, 23, 27

SCOTTISH NATIONAL GALLERY

nationalgalleries.org

The National Gallery shop has gifts, prints, jewelry, books and postcards. Lots of designs from the gallery's collection.

➕ D6 ✉ The Mound EH2 2EL ☎ 0131 624 6200 🚌 3, 10, 17, 23, 24, 27, 44; free gallery bus

STEWART CHRISTIE & CO.

stewart-christie.com

Bespoke tailors for more than 200 years, Stewart Christie & Co. make garments on the premises. This family business provides country and formal clothing, including Scottish tweed jackets, moleskin trousers, Highland dress and tartan evening trousers.

➕ B5 ✉ 63 Queen Street EH2 4NA ☎ 0131 225 6639 🚌 12, 13, 15, 23, 27, 29, 42

TISO

tiso.com

Helpful staff offer knowledgeable advice on the quality outdoor clothing and equipment they sell here—all you need for walking, climbing, camping or skiing, and there is also a good mountaineering and travel book section.

➕ C5 ✉ 123–125 Rose Street EH2 3DT

☎ 0131 225 9486 🚌 13, 23, 27, 29

VALVONA & CROLLA

valvonacrolla.co.uk

This much-loved deli has hardly changed since opening in 1934.

Shelves are stacked with the finest Italian produce and wines. Mozzarella is shipped from Naples, an array of cured meats hang from the ceiling, and bread is baked on site daily.

➕ F3 ✉ 19 Elm Row EH7 4AA ☎ 0131 556 6066 🚌 7, 10, 11, 12, 14, 16

WATERSTONE'S

waterstones.com

Edinburgh has several branches of this leading bookshop. The one at the west end of Princes Street spreads over several floors, with large windows and a café on the top level that gives great views to the castle. More branches are at the east end of Princes Street, as well as George Street and Ocean Terminal.

➕ B6 ✉ 128 Princes Street EH2 4AD

☎ 0131 226 2666 🚌 3, 10, 17, 23, 24, 27, 44

WAVERLEY MALL

waverleymall.com

You'll find the city's main post office, a currency exchange bureau, a supermarket, food court and more than 20 stores in this multilevel mall (formerly Princes Mall) next to Waverley Station. Edinburgh's main tourist information system is at street level.

➕ E5 ✉ Princes Street EH1 1BQ ☎ 0131 557 3759 🚌 3, 22, 23, 25, 27, 29

Entertainment and Nightlife

AMARONE

amaronerestaurant.co.uk

This stylish wine bar and restaurant in the heart of New Town has a good wine list and an Italian-inspired cocktail list.

🚇 D5 ⊠ 13 St. Andrew Square EH2 2BH
☎ 0131 523 1171 🕐 Mon–Fri 8am–10.30pm, Sat–Sun 10am–10.30pm 🚌 8, 10, 11, 12, 16 or tram to St. Andrew Square

ASSEMBLY ROOMS

assemblyroomsedinburgh.com

The elegant Georgian Assembly Rooms showcase mainstream Festival Fringe productions, with an impressive ball-room and music hall.

🚇 C5 ⊠ 54 George Street EH2 2LE ☎ 0131 220 4348 (box office) 🚌 24, 29, 42

BAILIE BAR

thebailiebar.co.uk

Sample real ales at this New Town basement pub with an interesting trian-gular-shape bar and low ceilings.

🚇 B3 ⊠ 2–4 St. Stephen Street EH3 5AL
☎ 0131 225 4673 🕐 Mon–Thu 11am–mid-night, Fri–Sat 11am–1am, Sun 12.30–midnight 🚌 19A, 24, 29, 42

LGBT

Edinburgh has a vibrant scene that revolves around Broughton Street, an area known as the Pink Triangle. Hotels, clubs, cafés and pubs cater to the gay community. For pre-club drinks try The Basement (⊠ 10a–12a Broughton Street EH1 3RH ☎ 0131 557 0097; basement-bar-edinburgh.co.uk) or The Street (⊠ 2b Picardy Place EH1 3JT ☎ 0131 556 4272; thestreetbaredinburgh.co.uk). CC Blooms (⊠ 23 Greenside Place EH1 3AA ☎ 0131 556 9331), is a popular gay rendezvous during the day and turns into a lively club-style venue at night, open till 3am.

THE BARONY

This fine old pub serves decent food and hosts live rock and blues most Saturday and Sunday nights.

🚇 E3 ⊠ 81–85 Broughton Street EH1 3RJ
☎ 0131 558 2873 🕐 Normal pub hours; live shows from 8.30 🚌 8

BOURBON BAR

bourbonedin.com

Opened in 2016, this venue combines a lounge bar with two separate club rooms that host a variety of club nights. In the basement, Ninja Kitchen (▷ 85) serves Asian-fusion tapas.

🚇 C5 ⊠ 24 Frederick Street EH2 2JR
☎ 0131 202 6406 🕐 Daily until 3am (1am Tue and Sun); food until 9pm 🚌 12, 19, 36, 37, 41, 43

CAFÉ ROYAL

caferoyaledinburgh.co.uk

Stop for a drink and admire the ornate ceiling, tiled portraits, stained glass and mahogany carvings here. The huge bar takes center stage.

🚇 E5 ⊠ 19 West Register Street EH2 2AA
☎ 0131 556 1884 🕐 Mon–Wed 11–11, Thu 11am–midnight, Fri–Sat 11am–1am, Sun 12.30–11pm 🚌 3, 10, 17, 23, 24, 27, 44

EDINBURGH PLAYHOUSE

livenationtheatres.co.uk

Big-budget musicals, dance shows and visiting rock bands make good use of this multipurpose auditorium close to the east end of Princes Street.

🚇 F4 ⊠ 18–22 Greenside Place EH1 3AA
☎ 0131 524 3333 🚌 7, 10, 11, 12, 14, 22, 25, 26, 49

JONGLEURS

jongleurs.com

With more than 30 years' experience chalked up, and a constant stream of

well-known comedians passing through its doors, the Edinburgh branch of this chain of comedy clubs is always good for a laugh.

🔲 F4 ✉ Unit 6/7 Omni Centre, Greenside Place EH1 3AA ☎ 0131 524 9300 (for bookings) ⏰ Times vary 🚌 7, 10, 11, 12, 14, 22, 25, 26

LOLA LO

lolalo.co.uk

This Polynesian-style tiki bar and club has a list of some 30 potent cocktails and also serves fine champagnes and rums from around the world. It attracts a young, lively and free-spending clientele.

🔲 C5 ✉ 43B Frederick Street EH2 1EP ☎ 0131 226 2224 ⏰ Thu 10.30pm–3am, Fri–Sat 10pm–3am 🚌 24, 29, 42

LULU

luluedinburgh.co.uk

Tucked beneath the Tigerlily Hotel, Lulu is glamorous and fashionable—its weekly hip-hop and Dirty Sexy nights are filled to capacity.

LICENSING LAWS

Edinburgh's bars, pubs, restaurants and cafés serve alcohol from 11am until 11pm (and often later, especially on Friday and Saturday nights). Some bars and restaurants allow diners to bring their own wine or beer (but not spirits), but may charge a corkage fee. Supplying alcohol to people under 18 is a criminal offense. Families with children are accepted in most restaurants and cafés, but kids are less welcome in pubs, especially in the evenings. The ban on smoking indoors accidentally created a brand-new sidewalk culture, and many bars and cafés now have tables outside where smokers can indulge their addiction.

🔲 B5 ✉ 125 George Street EH2 4JN ☎ 0131 225 5005 ⏰ Daily 8pm–3am 🚌 13, 19, 37, 41

OPAL LOUNGE

opallounge.co.uk

This multipurpose basement space is stylish but casual. Dance to funky, soul-infused tunes.

🔲 C5 ✉ 51a George Street EH2 2HT ☎ 0131 226 2275 ⏰ Sun–Thu 10pm–3am, Fri, Sat 9pm–3am 🚌 13, 23, 24, 27, 29, 42

RICK'S

ricksedinburgh.co.uk

Rick's is a sophisticated cocktail bar, restaurant, breakfast café and boutique hotel all in one.

🔲 C5 ✉ 55A Frederick Street EH2 1LH ☎ 0131 622 7800 ⏰ Daily 7.30am–1am 🚌 24, 29

ROSS OPEN AIR THEATRE

This is an impressive spot for a busy summer schedule of outdoor concerts and live events, right beneath Edinburgh Castle.

🔲 C6 ✉ Princes Street Gardens EH2 2HG ☎ 0131 228 8616 🚌 3, 10, 17, 23, 24, 27, 44

SHANGHAI

lemondehotel.co.uk

In the basement of Le Monde hotel, this state-of-the-art club prides itself on being Edinburgh's top late-night venue.

🔲 D5 ✉ 16 George Street EH2 2PF ☎ 0131 270 3900 ⏰ Daily 10pm–3am 🚌 13, 19, 37, 41

THE STAND

thestand.co.uk

This basement venue is pivotal to the Scottish stand-up comedy circuit and has spawned spin-offs in Glasgow and Newcastle. During the Edinburgh Fringe

it hosts comedy in its original premises and at several nearby spaces. The rest of the year it presents a mixture of established comedians and new talent seven nights a week.

🔲 E4 ✉ 5 York Place EH1 3EB ☎ 0131 558 7272 🕐 Mon–Sat 7.30pm–1am, Sun 12.30–midnight 🚌 10, 11, 12, 15, 16, 17, 26, 44

STUDIO 24

Billing itself proudly as "not for the mainstream," this independent venue plays host to live music and club nights that celebrate every alternative genre from punk and new wave to rockabilly, ska, garage and psychedelia.

🔲 G5 ✉ 24–26 Calton Road EH8 8DP ☎ 0131 558 3758 🕐 Fri–Sat 10pm–5am (opening times may vary) 🚌 15, 35, 113

VUE CINEMA

myvue.com

A huge glass-fronted building opposite John Lewis, this multiplex cinema has stadium seating and the latest in digital surround sound. There are 12 screens, of which three come with Gold Class—luxury leather seats, waiter bar service during the film and a wall-to-wall screen.

🔲 F4 ✉ Omni Centre, Greenside Place EH1 3AA (book online) 🚌 7, 10, 11, 12, 14, 22, 25, 26

Where to Eat

BELL'S DINER (£–££)

bellsdineredinburgh.co.uk

Bell's hasn't changed its formula for more than 40 years. This little gem has been serving classic burgers and steaks smothered with your own choice of sauce in the heart of bohemian Stockbridge since the 1970s. It may not be the most trendy but it's easy to see why it has such a loyal local following.

🔲 B3 ✉ 7 St. Stephen Street EH3 5AN ☎ 0131 225 8116 🕐 Mon 5–9, Tue–Fri 5–10, Sat 12–10, Sun 3–9.30 🚌 19A, 24, 29, 42

LE CAFÉ ST. HONORÉ (££)

cafesthonore.com

Enjoy intimate, relaxed dining in a French-style restaurant serving a fine blend of Scottish and French dishes.

🔲 C5 ✉ 34 NW Thistle Street Lane EH2 1EA ☎ 0131 226 2211 🕐 Mon–Fri 12–2, 5.15–10, Sat–Sun 12–2, 6–10 🚌 23, 27, 29, 41

CONTINI RISTORANTE (££)

contini.com

Edinburgh abounds with Italian restaurants—some venerable and old-school,

---

EATING ITALIAN

Large numbers of Italians emigrated to Scotland in the early 20th century, bringing with them their own culinary influences. Hence, you will find many good Italian restaurants, mostly in Edinburgh's West End.

some on trend. Family-run Contini occupies the middle ground, with classic pasta dishes given a modern spin and a menu that focuses on a different Italian region every month.

C5 · 103 George Street EH2 3ES · 0131 225 1550 · Mon–Fri 8am–10.30pm, Sat 11–10.30, Sun 11–9 · 24, 29, 42

DISHOOM (£££)

dishoom.com/edinburgh

This bustling restaurant opened in 2016 in a historic building on the south side of St. Andrew Square. Its menu, redolent of the spices of South Asia, brought fabulous Irani Bombay street food to Edinburgh and has proved an instant hit.

E5 · 3a St. Andrew Square EH2 2BD · 0131 202 6406 · Mon–Wed 8am–11pm, Thu–Fri 8am–midnight, Sat 9am–midnight, Sun 9am–11pm · 2, 8, 9, 10, 11, 12, 16, 25, 26, 41 or tram to St. Andrew Square

THE DOGS (££)

thedogsonline.co.uk

Rave reviews welcomed this exciting new addition to Edinburgh's restaurant

---

DINE WITH A VIEW

For fine food and spectacular views try the Forth Floor Restaurant at Harvey Nichols (✉ 30–34 St. Andrew Square EH2 2AD · ☎ 0131 524 8350), which has a balcony and floor-to-ceiling windows providing striking views of the Castle in one direction and the Firth of Forth in the other. The Tower Restaurant (▷ 44) is located on the fifth floor of the National Museum of Scotland (▷ 27) and offers superb views of the Castle, the incredible skyline of the Royal Mile and over Old Town. This is rooftop dining at its best. The Starbank Inn (▷ 106) looks out over the Firth of Forth to Fife.

---

scene. The bustling first-floor venue is a great place to try the likes of cauliflower cheese soup followed by liver and bacon with sweet-and-sour onions.

D4 · 110 Hanover Street EH2 1DR · 0131 220 1208 · Daily 11–11 · 13, 19, 23, 27, 41, 42, 45

DOME (£££)

thedomeedinburgh.com

The Dome is a classy venue in a converted bank with a magnificent glass dome as the focal point. Classic Scottish cuisine is blended with European and Far Eastern tastes. There's also a tea-room serving delicate sandwiches and sumptuous pastries.

D5 · 14 George Street EH2 2PF · 0131 624 8624 · Daily 10–late · 29, 42

EARTHY CANONMILLS (£–££)

earthy.co.uk

Earthy lives up to its name with a menu packed with locally sourced and organic ingredients. Part café, part restaurant, it serves such delights as orange-cured venison and surprising aromatic desserts. Beside the Water of Leith, it's handy for the Botanic Garden too.

C2 · 1–6 Canonmills Bridge EH3 5LF · 0131 556 9696 · Café daily 9–5; restaurant Tue–Sat 6pm–midnight · 8

EDEN'S KITCHEN (£)

edens-kitchen.com

This bistro serves mezes and main courses, pasta, pizza and burgers, and offers an above-average kids' menu. Eden's Kitchen has a bring-your-own alcohol policy and, conveniently, there's a good liquor store opposite.

E3 · 32c Broughton Street EH1 3SB · 0131 556 6588 · Daily 10–10 (open later Fri and Sat) · 8, 9 or tram to York Pace

EDUCATED FLEA (££)

educatedflea.co.uk

Educated Flea serves Asian-fusion dishes such as sticky soy and star anise beef and spicy tempura brisket, plus an array of Scottish-influenced starters and main courses.

🔳 E3 ✉ 32b Broughton Street EH1 3SB ☎ 0131 556 8092 🕐 Mon–Fri 12–2.30, 5–10, Sat 10–10, Sun 10–9 🚌 8, 9 or tram to York Place

LA GARRIGUE (£££)

lagarrigue.co.uk

A showcase for food from the Languedoc region in France, the hearty Gallic cooking is presented with finesse and the wines and cheeses are also from the region. With the dominant blue tint and the wooden furniture, there is a strong Mediterranean feel.

🔳 F6 ✉ 31 Jeffrey Street EH1 1DH ☎ 0131 557 3032 🕐 Daily 12–2.30, 6–9.30 🚌 23, 35, 36

GUSTO (££)

gustorestaurants.uk.com

Modern Italian cuisine using traditional methods can be found at this stylish restaurant on one of Edinburgh's busiest streets. Black-and-white photographs adorn the walls and sleek furniture completes the picture. Enjoy tasty pizzas from the open fire.

🔳 B5 ✉ 135 George Street EH2 4JH ☎ 0131 225 2555 🕐 Sun–Thu 12–10, Fri–Sat 11–11 🚌 13, 19, 37, 41

HOWIES (£)

howies.uk.com

In a delightful 200-year-old Georgian building, this restaurant offers fresh Scottish produce such as haggis, hot-smoked salmon and steak, served with imagination at a good price. There is

another branch of Howies at 10–14 Victoria Street.

🔳 F5 ✉ 29 Waterloo Place EH1 3BQ ☎ 0131 556 5766 🕐 Daily 12–2.30, 5.30–10 🚌 8, 29, 37, 37a

KWEILIN (££)

kweilin.net

Enjoy beautifully cooked traditional Cantonese cuisine in plush surround-ings. The menu offers a great selection, and there is an excellent wine list.

🔳 C4 ✉ 19–21 Dundas Street EH3 6QG ☎ 0131 557 1875 🕐 Tue–Thu 12–2, 5.30–10.30, Fri–Sat 12–2, 5.30–11 🚌 23, 27

MUSSEL INN (££)

mussel-inn.com

The tastiest shellfish, scallops and oysters are delivered fresh from the Scottish sea lochs to this bustling eatery in the heart of New Town.

🔳 C5 ✉ 61–65 Rose Street EH2 2NH ☎ 0843 289 2481 (calls cost 7p a minute) 🕐 Mon–Thu 12–3, 5.30–10, Fri–Sun 12.30–10 🚌 3, 12, 29, 44

NINJA KITCHEN AT BOURBON BAR AND LOUNGE (££)

Cosmopolitan Ninja Kitchen serves zingy dishes influenced by the cuisine of

South and East Asia, from Malaysian *rendang* to Thai *tom yam* and Taiwanese *gua bao* buns. It's in a basement beneath fashionable Bourbon Bar—perfect for after-dinner drinks.

➕ C5 ✉ 24 Frederick Street EH2 2JR
☎ 0131 322 3190 🕐 Daily 12–9 🚌 12, 19, 31, 36, 37, 41, 43

OLIVE BRANCH (££)

theolivebranchscotland.co.uk
A trendy mix of black leather, wicker and velour seating in neutral shades blends well with the wooden floors and bare brick walls. Large windows enable serious people-watching in an area that is popular with the wild and bold.

➕ E3 ✉ 91 Broughton Street EH1 3RX
☎ 0131 557 8589 🕐 Mon–Fri 11.45–10, Sat–Sun 10–10 🚌 8, 17

LA P'TITE FOLIE (££)

laptitefolie.co.uk
The French cuisine more than measures up to the outstanding Tudor building housing this cheerful eatery, where the tables are rather close together. There is a second branch at 61 Frederick Street.

➕ A5 ✉ Tudor House, 9 Randolph Place EH3 7TE ☎ 0131 225 8678 🕐 Mon–Thu 12–3, 6–10, Fri–Sat 12–3, 6–11 🚌 13, 19, 36, 37, 41

THE REFINERY (££)

drakeandmorgan.co.uk/the-refinery
This bright, modern brasserie and cocktail bar on the south side of St. Andrew Square serves a menu that ranges from eggs Benedict and chicken satay to prawn lollipops, fish and chips and lemon chicken. It has tables outside for sunny days.

➕ D5 ✉ 5 St. Andrew Square EH2 2BD
☎ 0333 210 0117 🕐 Mon–Fri 8am–midnight, Sat 9am–1am, Sun 10–7 🚌 2, 8, 9, 10, 11, 12, 16, 25, 26, 41 or tram to St. Andrew Square

RESTAURANT MARK GREENAWAY (£££)

markgreenaway.com
Celebrity chef Mark Greenaway is known for his beautifully presented dishes, all made from fresh, local ingredients. His signature slow-roast pork is to die for, as are the desserts.

➕ B5 ✉ 69 N Castle Street EH2 3LJ
☎ 0131 226 1155 🕐 Tue–Sat 12–2.30, 5.30–10 🚌 24, 29, 42

SMOKE STACK (££)

smokestack.org.uk
Fabulous steaks, huge portions, reasonable prices and a great location make Smoke Stack a guaranteed pleaser. Nothing fancy; just great food, well prepared.

➕ E3 ✉ 53–55 Broughton Street EH1 3RJ
☎ 0131 556 6032 🕐 Daily 11–11 🚌 8

THE SPICE PAVILION (£)

thespicepavilion.co.uk
This New Town restaurant is a cut above many of Edinburgh's Asian curry houses. Great *puris* and delicious, fluffy Indian breads will tantalize your taste buds.

➕ C4 ✉ 31a Dundas Street EH3 6QG
☎ 0131 467 5506 🕐 Daily 12–1.30, 5.30–10 🚌 23, 24, 27, 29

VINCAFFÈ (££)

valvonacrolla.co.uk
The owners of Scotland's oldest delicatessen, Valvona & Crolla (▷ 80), opened this café/wine bar to create a Continental-style meeting place. Their own finest ingredients are used to provide simple or sophisticated Italian food, washed down by a glass of wine from their range.

➕ E4 ✉ 11 Multrees Walk EH1 3DQ
☎ 0131 557 0088 🕐 Mon–Sat 7.30am–late, Sun 10am–late 🚌 8, 10, 11, 12, 16

There's plenty to see right on the doorstep of the city and the transport is good. From award-winning Edinburgh Zoo to the Royal Yacht *Britannia* at Leith, the attractions are well worth a visit.

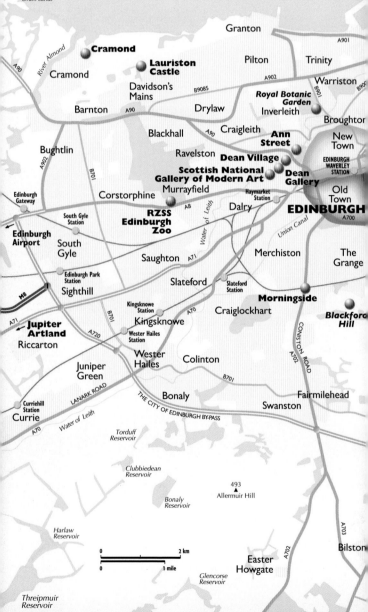

Firth of Forth

Royal Yacht
Britannia

Leith

A199

A900

Meadowbank

A1140

B6415

Portobello

Dumbiedykes

Holyrood Park
251
▲ Arthur's Seat

Northfield

Fisherrow Sands

A1

Bingham

Brunstane
Station

Fisherrow

Duddingston

Brunstane

Musselburgh

Prestonfield

A6095

Craigmillar

Newcraighall
Station

Musselburgh
Station

Stoneybank

Craigmillar
Castle

A6106

The
Inch

MILLERHILL ROAD

B6415

A701

Moredun

A7

Danderhall

A720

Liberton

GILMERTON ROAD

OLD DALKEITH ROAD

THE CITY OF EDINBURGH BY-PASS

Gracemount

ROAD

*Dalkeith
Park*

A720

A772

Dalkeith

Loanhead

A768

River North Esk

Lasswade

A7

River South Esk

A701

A768

Bonnyrigg

A6094

B703

B7006

Newtongrange

Roslin

B6392

B704

Craigmillar Castle

HIGHLIGHTS

● Views
● Substantial ruins
● Queen Mary's Room
● Former chapel and dovecote

TIP

● Don't be put off by the journey to the castle through some of Edinburgh's less admired housing developments—it's worth the effort.

The ruins of one of Scotland's most impressive 15th-century tower houses are particularly pleasant to visit when the hustle and bustle of Edinburgh becomes too much.

Splendid remains Craigmillar lies 4km (2.5 miles) southeast of the heart of the city and is often overlooked because of the more famous Edinburgh Castle. At its core is a well-preserved early-15th-century L-plan tower house with walls up to 2.7m (9ft) thick, constructed on the site of an older fortification by Sir George Preston. The main defensive features—massive doors, a spiral turnpike stair (connecting three floors), narrow passageways and two outer walls to fend off English attackers—make it a great place to explore.

Surprisingly rural considering its proximity to the city, Craigmillar Castle makes a pleasant alternative for an afternoon out

Fit for a queen Mary, Queen of Scots, fled here on several occasions when the pressures of life at Holyrood became too great, notably after the murder of her secretary and darling David Rizzio in 1566, and the tiny chamber where she slept bears her name. It is said that during this stay conspirators agreed to the "Craigmillar Bond," the plot to kill Lord Darnley, Mary's unscrupulous and unpopular husband.

Falling into ruin Craigmillar was bought from the Prestons by Sir John Gilmour in 1660 with the intention to convert it into a fashionable residence. The family, however, decided to move to Inch House at Gilmerton instead and Craigmillar was abandoned. Overgrown and ruinous, it was acquired by the state in 1946, and is now in the hands of Historic Scotland.

THE BASICS

historicenvironment.scot

🗺 See map ▷ 89

✉ Craigmillar Castle Road EH16 4SY

☎ 0131 661 4445

🕐 Apr–Sep daily 9.30–5.30; Oct daily 9.30–4.30; Nov–Mar Sat–Wed 9.30–4.30

🚌 2, 14

♿ Poor, but access to visitor area

✋ Inexpensive

Leith

HIGHLIGHTS

- The Shore
- Ocean Terminal
- Water of Leith Visitor Centre
- Royal Yacht *Britannia*

TIP

- Choose a dry and, if possible, sunny day to visit Leith to get the most from the coastal location.

Edinburgh's seaport, amalgamated with the city in 1921, has been a dock area since the 14th century. Following a decline in shipbuilding, it has been regenerated into a tourist area.

New role Leith was for many years a prosperous town in its own right. As the shipbuilding industry began to wane in the 20th century the town went into decline, but it has come up in the world again and now it buzzes with fashionable eating places. The area known as The Shore, along the waterfront, is filled with flourishing bars and restaurants. Warehouses, once full of wine and whisky, have been converted into smart accommodations. Where Tower Street meets The Shore, look for the Signal Tower, built in 1686 as a windmill.

Edinburgh's river, the Water of Leith, flows through the middle of the town and the visitor center tells more about its heritage.

Historic Leith The town has witnessed its share of history—Mary, Queen of Scots, landed here from France in 1561 and reputedly stayed at Andro Lamb's House, in Water Street. King James II banned golf from Leith Links as it interfered with archery practice. The original 13 rules of golf were drawn up here in 1744, but in 1907 the dunes were flattened to create a public park and golf was banned once more.

Modern town For visitors, the Royal Yacht *Britannia* (▷ 95) is the main draw, as well as the Ocean Terminal Centre, one of Europe's largest shopping and leisure complexes.

THE BASICS

➕ See map ▷ 89
✉ Leith
🚌 1, 11, 16, 22, 34, 35, 36
ℹ VisitScotland, 94 Ocean Drive EH6 6JH
☎ 0131 472 2222

Royal Botanic Garden

TOP 25

The entrance gate to the gardens (left) and an orchid from the collection (right)

THE BASICS

rbge.org.uk
🔲 B1
✉ 20A Inverleith Row
EH3 5LR
☎ 0131 552 7171
🕐 Apr–Sep daily 10–7;
Mar, Oct daily 10–6;
Nov–Feb daily 10–4
🍴 Gateway Restaurant
and Terrace Café
🚌 8, 17, 23, 27
♿ Good
💷 Entry to garden free;
glasshouses inexpensive;
tours moderate
❓ Tours lasting around
90 minutes leave West
Gate at 11 and 2, Apr–Sep.
Gift shop stocks stationery,
plants and related
souvenirs

HIGHLIGHTS

● Rock Garden
● Glasshouses
● Tropical Aquatic House
● Chinese Hillside
● Scottish Heath Garden
● The gates
● Orchid and Cycad House
● Woodland Garden

Known locally as The Botanics, these gardens boast some 15,500 species, one of the largest collections of living plants in the world. It's possibly Edinburgh's finest recreational asset.

City greenery Occupying this site since 1823, the gardens cover more than 28ha (69 acres) of beautifully landscaped and wooded grounds to the north of the city, forming an immaculately maintained green oasis. You can walk to the garden from Princes Street via Stockbridge, though you may wish to take the bus back up the hill.

Inside or out? There are 10 glasshouses to explore, offering a perfect haven on cold days. They include an amazingly tall palm house dating back to 1834, and the Tropical Aquatic House, with its giant waterlilies and an underwater view of fish swimming through the lily roots. Outside, the plants of the Chinese Hillside and the Scottish Heath Garden are particularly interesting, and in summer the herbaceous borders are breathtaking. Check out the rhododendron collection and the Rock Garden, which displays some 5,000 species and is best seen in May. The highest point of the garden has a fine view of the city.

Striking design The West Gate, or Carriage Gate, is the main entrance, but don't miss the stunning inner east side gates, designed by local architect Ben Tindall in 1996.

Royal Yacht *Britannia*

The Royal Yacht Britannia *(left)* has a full-size lounge within its hull *(right)*

This former royal yacht is one of the world's most famous ships, now moored in Edinburgh's historic port of Leith. It is 83rd in a long line of royal yachts stretching back to 1660.

New role *Britannia* was decommissioned in 1997 after a cut in government funds. It had carried the Queen and her family on 968 official voyages all over the world since its launch at Clydebank in 1953.

Vital statistics For 40 years, *Britannia* served the royal family, sailing more than 1 million miles to become the most famous ship in the world. A compact yacht, it is just 125.6m (412ft) long. It carried a crew of 240, including a Royal Marine band and an additional 45 household staff when the royal family were aboard. A self-guided tour using handsets takes you around the yacht itself. *Britannia* still retains the fittings and furnishings of her working days, which gives an intimate insight into the royals away from usual palace protocol.

Royal and naval precision Check out the apartments adorned with hundreds of original items from the royal collection. The grandest room is the State Dining Room, and the most elegant the Drawing Room. Imagine the royal family relaxing in the Sun Lounge and view the modest sleeping quarters. Everything on board is shipshape, from the Engine Room to the fully equipped Sick Bay.

THE BASICS

royalyachtbritannia.co.uk
✚ See map ▷ 89
✉ Ocean Terminal, Leith EH6 6JJ
☎ 0131 555 5566
🕐 Jul–Sep daily 9.30–4.30; Apr–Jun, Oct daily 9.30–4; Jan–Mar, Nov–Dec daily 10–3.30
🍴 Cafés and restaurants in Ocean Terminal
🚌 1, 11, 22, 34, 35, 36
♿ Excellent
💷 Expensive
❓ Reservations strongly advised in high season

HIGHLIGHTS

● Royal Apartments
● Drawing Room
● State Dining Room
● Sun Lounge
● Royal Bedrooms
● Sick Bay and Operating Theatre
● Engine Room
● The Bridge

RZSS Edinburgh Zoo

TOP
25

HIGHLIGHTS

● Giant and red pandas
● Walkthrough exhibits
● Tiger Tracks enclosure
● Penguin Parade

TIP

● To see the giant pandas you need a separate timed ticket. This is free but spaces are limited so book in advance.

Giant pandas Tian Tian and Yang Guang are the star attractions at RZSS Edinburgh Zoo, which promotes conservation while offering a great day out.

Conservation, education and fun RZSS Edinburgh Zoo is a world leader in breeding endangered species. It also campaigns to protect wildlife worldwide, while demonstrating how a visitor attraction can modernize to survive. Located at Corstorphine, 5km (3 miles) west of the city center, the zoo covers 33ha (82 acres) of wooded hillside and is home to around 1,000 animals.

Natural habitats New-generation exhibits allow visitors to encounter pelicans, wallabies and lemurs in walkthrough exhibits, and get

Clockwise from far left: on lookout, a meerkat stands guard at Edinburgh Zoo; Sumatran tiger Jambi arrived in 2015; one of zoo's two giant pandas; 18th-century Mansion House, at the heart of the zoo, is a popular venue for functions; gentoo penguins on parade

close to big cats through a glass tunnel that runs through the Tiger Tracks enclosure. There's also an aerial walkway across rolling hillocks occupied by byala antelope, and the Budongo Trail, where you can see chimpanzees in a unique interactive enclosure.

Pandas and penguins Tian Tian (female) and Yang Guang (male), on loan from China, are the only giant pandas in Britain. Pandas are solitary creatures, so they are kept in separate enclosures. The zoo also hopes that its red pandas, Bruce and Ginger, which arrived in 2016 and 2017, will breed. Penguin Rock is Europe's largest penguin pool, complete with waterfall, and the Penguin Parade, when penguins waddle around the enclosure with their keepers, is a daily highlight.

THE BASICS

edinburghzoo.org.uk
⊞ See map ▷ 88
✉ Corstorphine Road
EH12 6TS
☎ 0131 334 9171
🕐 Apr–Sep daily 9–6;
Oct, Mar daily 9–5;
Nov–Feb daily 9–4.30
🍴 Restaurant, café, kiosks
and picnic areas
🚌 12, 26, 31
♿ Very good
💷 Expensive

Scottish National Gallery of Modern Art

TOP 25

Outside the gallery; Le Coureur (The Runner), by Germaine Richier

THE BASICS

nationalgalleries.org
➕ See map ▷ 88
✉ 75 Belford Road EH4 3DR
☎ 0131 624 6200
🕐 Daily 10–5
🍴 Gallery Café
🚌 13; free bus links all five national galleries
🚉 Edinburgh Haymarket
♿ Very good
💷 Free, but may be charges for temporary exhibitions
❓ Shop stocks books, cards and gifts

HIGHLIGHTS

● Works by the Scottish Colourists, including those by John Duncan Fergusson
● Major works by Picasso, Matisse and Lichtenstein
● Sculptures by Henry Moore and Barbara Hepworth
● Works by contemporary artists, including Damien Hirst and Rachel Whiteread
● Eduard Paolozzi's studio

The gallery opened at this parkland site in 1984, providing an ideal setting for the work of those who have been in the forefront of modern art: Matisse, Picasso, Hirst. You'll find them all here.

Setting the scene The first thing you see as you arrive at the main gallery is a sweeping, living sculpture of grassy terraces and semi-circular ponds, an installation called *Landform UEDA* by Charles Jencks. After such a grand introduction the rest of the gallery seems quite small, but it is large in terms of its enviable collection of modern art from around the world. It is housed in a former school.

On display Regularly changing exhibitions occupy the first floor, with a varied display from the gallery's collection on the second floor. Look for works by Picasso, Braque and Matisse, Hepworth and Gabo. The work of the early 20th-century group of painters known as the Scottish Colourists is particularly striking, with canvases by Samuel John Peploe (1871–1935), John Duncan Fergusson (1874–1961) and F.C.B. Cadell (1883–1937). Also of interest are Fergusson's dramatic *Portrait of Anne Estelle Rice* (c.1908), the vibrancy of Cadell's *The Blue Fan* (c.1922) and Peploe's later, more fragmentary work, such as *Iona Landscape, Rocks* (c.1927).

More art Stroll across the road to the Dean Gallery (▷ 99), an outstation of the gallery.

ANN STREET

The estate built in 1814 by artist Sir Henry Raeburn in memory of his wife, Ann, is one of Edinburgh's most exclusive addresses. The houses combine classic splendor with cottagey charm.

🔲 A4 ✉ Ann Street 🚌 29, 37, 41, 42

BLACKFORD HILL

roe.ac.uk

One of Edinburgh's seven hills, the view from here is excellent. Just 3km (2 miles) south of central Edinburgh, it is home to the Royal Observatory, Edinburgh, which moved here from Calton Hill in 1895. The visitor area is open only for group visits and occasional events. There are Friday evening viewing sessions (book in advance; tel 0131 668 8404).

🔲 See map ▷ 88 ✉ Blackford 🚌 24, 38, 41 ♿ Few

CRAMOND

There are Roman remains, 16th-century houses, a fine church, an old inn and some elegant Victorian villas to hold your attention in this attractive suburb on the shores of the Firth of Forth. The Cramond Heritage Trust has a permanent exhibition in the Maltings exploring the history of the village. Take one of the good walks around the area or visit Lauriston Castle (▷ 100), nearby.

🔲 See map ▷ 88 ✉ Cramond ⏰ Maltings: Apr–Sep Sat–Sun 2–5; every afternoon during Festival 🚌 24, 41

DEAN GALLERY

Across the road from the Scottish National Gallery of Modern Art (▷ 98), this gallery is housed in a former orphanage and displays an excellent collection based around the work of Dada and the Surrealists, and the Scottish sculptor Eduard Paolozzi (b.1924).

🔲 See map ▷ 88 ✉ 73 Belford Road EH4 3DR ☎ 0131 624 6200 ⏰ Daily 10–5 🚌 13; free bus linking main galleries 🚆 Edinburgh Haymarket ♿ Very good 💷 Free

Take in the view over Edinburgh from Blackford Hill

Rows of boats at Cramond waterside

DEAN VILLAGE

The northern limit of New Town is marked by Thomas Telford's 1832 Dean Bridge. It spans a steep gorge created by the Water of Leith. The workers' cottages, warehouses and mill buildings have been restored and Dean has become a desirable residential area. The cemetery is the resting place of many well-known locals, including the New Town architect William Playfair.

See map ▷ 88 ✉ Dean 🚌 13, 37, 41

JUPITER ARTLAND

jupiterartland.org

This cutting-edge collection of contemporary landscape art and installations includes works by Charles Jencks, Andy Goldsworthy and Ian Hamilton Finlay, scattered around a 40ha (100-acre) estate surrounding Bonnington House.

See map ▷ 88 ✉ Bonnington House, Steadings, Wilkiestone EH627 8BB ☎ 01506 889 900 🕐 May–Sep Thu–Sun 10–5 (Aug daily) 🚌 27 💷 Moderate

LAURISTON CASTLE

edinburghmuseums.org.uk

This "castle" is the epitome of Edwardian comfort and style, a gabled and turreted mansion overlooking the Firth of Forth near Cramond. Starting out as a simple tower house, it was renovated and extended several times and left to the City of Edinburgh in 1926 by William Robert Reid.

See map ▷ 88 ✉ 2A Cramond Road South, Davidson's Mains EH4 5QD ☎ 0131 336 2060 🕐 Apr–Oct Sat–Thu tours at 2; Nov–Mar Sat–Sun at 2. Grounds daily Apr–Sep 8–8; Oct–Mar daily 8–5 🚌 24 ♿ Poor 💷 Castle: inexpensive. Grounds: free

MORNINGSIDE

Immortalized in the accent of novelist Muriel Spark's Jean Brodie, this quiet, leafy suburb still houses the wealthy of the city in elegant Victorian villas. Stroll round its pleasant streets for civilized shopping and afternoon tea.

See map ▷ 88 ✉ Morningside 🚌 5, 11, 15, 15A, 16, 17, 23, 41

Buildings at Dean village, on the banks of the Water of Leith

Excursions

MURRAYFIELD

Developed around the 18th-century Murrayfield House, this western suburb is a pleasant district and popular with city commuters. Scottish rugby has made its home here and Murrayfield hosts games during the Six Nations championships. The stadium was built by the Scottish Football Union and opened in 1925. A £37 million redevelopment gave it a new look and the ground was reopened by the Princess Royal in 1994. Murrayfield once held the world record for the largest attendance at a rugby game. This was for the match when Scotland played Wales in the Five Nations (as it was then) in 1975, drawing an enormous crowd of just over 104,000. Scotland won 12–10, inflicting Wales' only defeat of the tournament. The stadium's current seating capacity is 67,500.

THE BASICS

Distance: 2km (1.5 miles)
Journey time: 20 minutes
Murrayfield Stadium
✉ Corstorphine Road EH12 5PJ
☎ 0131 346 5000; scottishrugby.org
♿ Good
🚌 12, 26, 31
❓ Stadium tours available Mon–Sat at 11 (also 2.30 Thu–Fri); expensive

NORTH BERWICK

Once a small fishing port, North Berwick, on the south side of the Firth of Forth to the east of Edinburgh, has developed into a lively holiday resort. Pleasure craft crowd the little port and its splendid Victorian and Edwardian architecture suggests prosperity. Golf is the number one attraction of the area dubbed the North Berwick Golf Coast and has been played here since the 17th century. The Scottish Seabird Centre uses the latest technology to take pictures of seabirds nesting on the nearby cliffs and islands, and there are interactive and multimedia displays to interest all the family, as well as boat trips from April to October. Behind the town is the cone of the North Berwick Law, a 187m-high (613ft) volcanic plug, which rewards hikers with fine views from the top over the Fife coastline to the Forth Road Bridge and Edinburgh Castle.

THE BASICS

Distance: 40km (25 miles)
Journey time: 30 minutes
🚆 From Waverley
ℹ Quality Street
☎ 01620 892197
Scottish Seabird Centre
✉ The Harbour, North Berwick EH39 4SS
☎ 01620 890202; seabird.org
🕐 Apr–Sep daily 10–6; Oct–Mar Mon–Fri 10–5, Sat–Sun 10–5.30 (closes 4.30 in Dec and Jan)
♿ Moderate

THE BASICS

rosslynchapel.com
Distance: 11km (7 miles)
Journey time: 1 hour
✉ Roslin EH25 9PU
☎ 0131 440 2159
🕐 Apr–Oct Mon–Sat
9.30–6, Sun 12–4.45;
Oct–Mar Mon–Sat 9.30–5,
Sun 12–4.45
♿ Moderate
🚌 15A (Lothian bus); 62
(First bus)

ROSSLYN CHAPEL

In a tiny mining village south of Edinburgh, this is the most mysterious building in Scotland, perched above Roslin Glen. Founded in 1446 by William St. Clair, Third Earl of Orkney, the church was to be a large cruciform structure, but only the choir was completed, along with sections of the east transept walls. It is linked with the Knights Templar and other secretive societies, and is even believed by some to be the hiding place of the Holy Grail. The chapel found increased fame through its connection with the best-selling 2003 novel *The Da Vinci Code* by Dan Brown and was a location in the movie adaptation. Inside is the finest example of medieval stone-carving in Scotland, if not Britain. The chapel remains in the hands of the St Clair family and is still a place of worship.

THE BASICS

Distance: 26km
(16 miles)
Journey time: 1 hour
🚆 From Waverley to
Dalmeny station
🚌 X4, 43 (First buses)
ℹ Forth Bridges Tourist
Information Centre,
Queensferry Lodge Hotel,
North Queensferry
☎ 01383 417759
Hopetoun House
✉ South Queensferry
EH30 9SL ☎ 0131 331
2451; hopetoun.co.uk
🕐 Easter–Sep daily
10.30–5 ♿ Expensive.
Grounds only: inexpensive

SOUTH QUEENSFERRY

From 1129 until 1964 a ferry operated across the Firth of Forth from South Queensferry; then the road suspension bridge opened. The distinctive red, cantilevered rail bridge built in the late 19th century has become an icon of Scotland and was declared a Unesco World Heritage Site in 2015. Only a short ride outside Edinburgh, this little royal burgh with its attractive clock tower (right) is a great place to come to admire the three (the Queensferry Crossing opened in 2017) Forth bridges on a summer's evening. To the west, Hopetoun House—which can only be reached easily by car—is a spectacular early 18th-century mansion built by William Bruce and William Adam. Home to the Marquis of Linlithgow, it is full of fine paintings, original furniture, tapestries and wonderful elaborate rococo detail. From the grounds there are more great views of the Forth bridges.

JUBILEE CLOCK 1887

Shopping

GOLDEN HARE BOOKS

goldenharebooks.com

This independent bookstore stocks a strong portfolio of intelligent fiction and nonfiction, beautifully illustrated editions, books for children and work by Edinburgh-based novelists and poets.

🗺 Off map ✉ 68 Stephen Street EH3 5AQ ☎ 0131 629 1396 🚌 24, 29, 42

HALIBUT AND HERRING

halibutandherring.co.uk

If you're looking for a gift that's different, head to this small shop in the attractive Bruntsfield district. There's a big selection of bathtime products, as well as funky jewelry, zany homeware, cute toys and unusual cards.

🗺 B9 ✉ 108 Bruntsfield Place E10 4ES ☎ 0131 229 2669 🚌 11, 15, 16, 17, 23

KINLOCH ANDERSON

kinlochanderson.com

While browsing for kilts, tartan trousers, jackets, skirts and accessories, you can learn more about the history of tartan from the experts on Highland dress since 1868.

🗺 Off map ✉ Commercial Street/Dock Street, Leith EH6 6EY ☎ 0131 555 1390 🚌 16, 22, 25, 36

LEITH MARKET

stockbridgemarket.com/leith

Like its parent in Stockbridge, this farmers' market's main stocks-in-trade are locally sourced produce and innovative, multinational street snacks. It hosts a special Vegan Quarter on the first Saturday of each month. You'll also find a choice of artisan-made clothes and accessories.

🗺 Off map ✉ Dock Place, Commercial Street EH6 6LU ☎ 0131 261 6181 🕐 Sat 10–4 (check website for changes) 🚌 22, 34

STOCKBRIDGE MARKET

stockbridgemarket.com

On the edge of the New Town, beside the Water of Leith, this Sunday food market is a great place to sample street food from all over the world or put together a picnic from stalls selling the best local (and often organic) produce. There are also artisan craft stalls of all kinds.

🗺 Off map ✉ 1 Saunders Street EH3 6TQ ☎ 0131 261 6181 🕐 Sun 10–5 (check website for changes) 🚌 24, 29, 42

THOSE WERE THE DAYS

thosewerethedaysvintage.com

Those Were The Days is a venerable St. Stephen Street institution. This is the place to go for pre-loved bridal wear, a perfect little black dress from the 1950s, a 1960s mini, 1970s flares and velvet jackets and accessories to match, for both men and women. All items are expertly cleaned and restored before going on sale.

🗺 Off map ✉ 26 St. Stephen Street EH3 5AL ☎ 0131 225 4400 🚌 24, 29, 42

HAGGIS

Haggis is Scotland's national dish and comes from an ancient recipe for using up the cheapest cuts of meat and traditionally eaten on Burns Night, 25 January. It's a sort of large mutton sausage based on the ground-up liver, lungs and heart of a sheep, mixed with oatmeal, onion and spices, and cooked up in the sheep's stomach. It can be dry, greasy or gritty, although when made properly can be delicious—a wee dram of whisky helps wash it down. These days restaurants serve their own spicy versions of the recipe, and if you want a small taster, you'll sometimes find it on the menu as a starter.

Entertainment and Nightlife

52 CANOES TIKI DEN

facebook.com/52canoes

52 Canoes brings a touch of the tropics to Edinburgh. Expect fruity (and impressively potent) rum-based cocktails served in novelty mugs. Themed party nights have an Aussie accent.

➕ Off map ✉ 13–14 Melville Street EH3 8DT
☎ 0131 226 4732 🚌 3, 4, 12, 25, 31, 33, 36

DOMINION

dominioncinemas.net

This old-fashioned, family-run cinema is the ideal antidote to the multiplex cinemas in the city. View latest releases in leather Pullman seats, or indulge in the Gold Class service, which offers leather sofas with complimentary wine or beer and snacks.

➕ Off map ✉ 18 Newbattle Terrace, Morningside EH10 4RT ☎ 0131 447 4771 (box office) 🚌 11, 15, 16, 23

FOOTBALL

Edinburgh's two main professional teams are Heart of Midlothian (Hearts) and Hibernian (Hibs), who play in the Scottish Premier League. They are at home on alternate Saturday afternoons Aug–May (reserve in advance).

Hearts FC ➕ Off map ✉ Tynecastle Stadium, McLeod Street EH11 2NL ☎ 0333 043 1874; heartsfc.co.uk 🚌 3, 3a, 25, 33

Hibs FC ➕ Off map ✉ Easter Road Stadium, 12 Albion Place EH7 5QG ☎ 0131 661 2159; hiberianfc.co.uk 🚌 1

LEITH DEPOT

leithdepot.com

This restaurant and bar in a former bus depot has its own 60-capacity venue and presents an eclectic array of live folk and rock, DJs and open mic nights. It's open four or five nights a week, often as late as 12.30.

➕ Off map ✉ 138–140 Leith Walk EH6 5DT
☎ 0131 555 4738 🚌 1, 19, 22, 25, 34

MUSSELBURGH RACECOURSE

musselburgh-racecourse.co.uk

Musselburgh Racecourse, one of the best small racecourses in Britain, hosts 27 flat and jump meetings a year, including family race days

➕ Off map ✉ Linkfield Road, Musselburgh, East Lothian EH21 7RG ☎ 0131 665 2859
🚌 15, 15A

ROYAL COMMONWEALTH POOL

edinburghleisure.co.uk

Edinburgh is proud of its Olympic-size indoor swimming pool, complete with a diving pool and waterslides. There's also a softplay on site for the under-10s.

➕ H9 ✉ 21 Dalkeith Road EH16 5BB
☎ 0131 667 7211 🚌 2, 14, 30, 33

RUGBY

(▷ 101 for Murrayfield.)

SUMMERHALL

summerhall.co.uk

This events venue and creative hub is one of Britain's largest. It hosts a wide range of events and performances, from stand-up comedy to traditional music performances, drama and cinema.

➕ Off map ✉ Summerhall Place EH9 1PL
☎ 0131 560 1580 🚌 41, 42

> **GOLF**
>
> Golf is the national game and with more than 500 courses throughout the country, it's no wonder fanatics flock to the area in pursuit of their first love. The closest courses can be found at Braids Hill, Craigmillar Park and Silverknowes. Visit scottishgolf.com for a list of courses in the area and a reservation service.

Where to Eat

PRICES	
Prices are approximate, based on a 3-course meal for one person.	
£££	over £25
££	£15–£25
£	under £15

CHOP CHOP (££)

chop-chop.co.uk

The all-you-can-eat feast at this Haymarket restaurant, where *jiaozi* dumplings, dim sum and the traditional, savory cuisine of northeast China rule, is one of Edinburgh's great eating bargains. You can bring your own wine or beer, which makes it an even better deal. The Haymarket location is handy for the Gallery of Modern Art.

➕ B7 ✉ 248 Morrison Street EH3 8DT ☎ 0131 221 1155 🕐 Mon–Fri 12–2, 5.30–10, Sat–Sun 1–3, 5–10 🚇 Haymarket 🚌 2, 3, 12, 31, 25, 26, 33, 100

FISHERS LEITH (££)

fishersrestaurants.co.uk

This zesty establishment, housed in a 17th-century watchtower, serves succulent fish in its brasserie-style dining room overlooking the Water of Leith.

➕ Off map ✉ 3 The Shore, Leith EH6 6QW ☎ 0131 553 5080 🕐 Daily 12–late 🚌 16, 22, 35, 36

RESTAURANT MARTIN WISHART (£££)

restaurantmartinwishart.co.uk

Michelin-starred Martin Wishart's dishes are beautifully presented at this tiny French restaurant on the waterfront at Leith. Bright, modern art stands out against the white walls and stone floors.

➕ Off map ✉ 54 The Shore, Leith EH6 6RA ☎ 0131 553 3557 🕐 Tue–Sat 12–2, 7–10 🚌 16, 22, 35, 36

RHUBARB (£££)

prestonfield.com

The food more than matches the opulent setting at this hotel. You will need to take a taxi to get here, but it's worth the effort.

➕ Off map ✉ Prestonfield Hotel, Priestfield Road EH16 5UT ☎ 0131 225 1333 🕐 Mon–Sat 12–2, 6–10, Sun 12.30–3, 6–10

THE SHIP ON THE SHORE (£££)

theshipontheshore.co.uk

Tasty seafood options at this bistro-style bar may include smoked salmon with lemon, chopped onion and capers, or paupiette of sole and prawns on braised leeks.

➕ Off map ✉ 24–26 The Shore, Leith EH6 6QN ☎ 0131 555 0409 🕐 Daily 9am–10pm 🚌 16, 22, 35, 36

STARBANK INN (££)

starbankinn-edinburgh.co.uk

Right on the waterfront, this inn offers traditional pub food, such as roast lamb with mint sauce, poached salmon, or chicken with tarragon cream sauce, and great views over the Firth of Forth.

➕ Off map ✉ 64 Laverockbank Road EH5 3BZ ☎ 0131 552 4141 🕐 Mon–Wed 11–11, Thu 11am–midnight, Fri–Sat 11am–1am, Sun 12–11 🚌 7, 10, 11, 16

TEUCHTERS LANDING (£££)

teuchtersbar.co.uk

This is a pretty quayside restaurant in a former lockkeeper's cottage. Fresh, well-prepared Scottish produce is crafted into the fish, meat and vegetarian dishes that are served in intimate booths or in the conservatory.

➕ Off map ✉ 1c Dock Place, Leith EH6 6LU ☎ 0131 554 7427 🕐 Daily 10.30–10 🚌 16, 22, 35, 36

Edinburgh has a diverse range of accommodations on offer, from opulent five-star hotels to lovely, if more humble, Georgian guesthouses. Scottish hospitality is in abundance throughout the city.

Introduction

Edinburgh is one of the world's favorite city-break destinations all year round. Reserving accommodations well in advance is recommended whenever you plan to travel, and essential if visiting during Festival season or over Hogmanay.

What the Grades Mean
You may notice that displayed outside all Scottish accommodation is a blue plaque with a thistle symbol. This indicates the star rating issued by VisitScotland (the Scottish Tourist Board). Every type of accommodation is assessed annually.

En Suite
Almost all hotels and guesthouses offer en-suite bathrooms, mostly with a tub.

Apartments
Edinburgh has a growing number of establishments offering self-catering studios and apartments for short-stay visitors. These can be excellent value, especially for families. Even in the city center there are plenty of supermarkets, delis and produce markets where you can buy all you need, from organic treats to microwave ready meals.

Paying
Most hotels will ask for a deposit or full payment in advance, especially for one-night bookings. Some will not take bookings for stays of only one night. Most hotels accept credit cards, but some smaller guesthouses or B&Bs may not, so check when booking.

WHEELCHAIR ACCESS

Planning and conservation limitations mean that some guesthouses and smaller boutique hotels within historic buildings are unable to provide elevators to upper floors or fully wheelchair-accessible rooms. Visitors who need wheelchair access will however find a wide choice of suitable accommodations in more recently built hotels all over Edinburgh, including the Old Town and New Town.

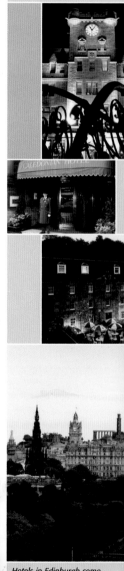

Hotels in Edinburgh come in many guises, often in beautiful old buildings

Budget Hotels

BONNINGTON GUEST HOUSE

thebonningtonguesthouse.com

The owners extend a warm welcome at this delightful Victorian house not far from Leith, with seven bedrooms finished to a high standard and retaining original features.

🟦 Off map ✉ 202 Ferry Road EH6 4NW ☎ 0131 554 7610 🚌 7, 11, 14

CASTLE VIEW GUEST HOUSE

castleviewgh.com

Few independent budget hotels in Edinburgh can match this 18-room guesthouse in a New Town Georgian town house for location or value for money. It offers convenient family rooms as well as doubles and twins, but note there is no elevator.

🟦 C5 ✉ 30 Castle Street EH2 3HT ☎ 0131 226 5784 🚌 12, 19, 31, 36, 37, 41, 43

DENE GUEST HOUSE

deneguesthouse.com

Hospitable owners offer a comfortable stay and a good breakfast at this clean and tidy Georgian town house. The New Town location makes it ideal for visiting the main sights.

🟦 C2 ✉ 7 Eyre Place EH3 5ES ☎ 0131 556 2700 🚌 23, 27, 36

ELDER YORK GUEST HOUSE

elderyork.co.uk

This charming guesthouse on the upper floors of a listed Georgian building offers superb value for money. You get a wee dram on the house on arrival, and the full Scottish breakfast will set you up for the day.

🟦 E3 ✉ 38 Elder Street EH1 3DX ☎ 0131 556 1926 🚌 10, 11, 12, 16, 26, 44 and tram

OLD WAVERLEY HOTEL

oldwaverley.co.uk

For visitors looking for an affordable, centrally located full-service hotel within easy walking distance of Waverley Station and many of Edinburgh's top attractions, the Old Waverley is hard to beat. Some rooms have views of the Scott Monument and the Castle.

🟦 D5 ✉ 43 Princes Street EH2 2BY ☎ 0131 556 4648 🚌 2, 3, 4, 12, 25, 26, 31, 33, 100 or tram to Princes Street

THE PLACE

yorkplace-edinburgh.co.uk

This boutique property offers contemporary luxury at rates that are within most budgets. Comfortable rooms and suites with power showers, orthopedic mattresses and luxury toiletries are complemented by a stylish cocktail lounge, restaurant and a covered terrace with a barbecue and big sports screen in summer.

🟦 E4 ✉ 34–38 York Place EH1 3HU ☎ 0131 556 7575 🚌 4, 10, 11, 12, 14, 16, 26, 41, 44, 45 or tram to York Place

YORK PLACE

28yorkplace.com

This small and friendly hotel in the heart of New Town has eight rooms, each with free WiFi, rainfall shower and tub. Deluxe and superior rooms have views across the New Town, and all rooms have handmade Scottish toiletries. There's a cozy lounge bar on the ground floor and a choice of continental or Scottish breakfast.

🟦 E4 ✉ 28 York Place EH1 3HU ☎ 0131 556 7575 🚌 4, 10, 11, 12, 14, 16, 26, 41, 44, 45 or tram to York Place

Mid-Range Hotels

12 PICARDY PLACE

twelvepicardyplace.com
This ultra-chic hotel in buzzy Broughton is less than 100 yards from York Place tram stop. Ten bedrooms are decorated in gray and cream, and the stone-floored bathrooms have soaking tubs and rainfall showers. The hotel has two restaurants and a bar with terrace.
➕ F4 ✉ 12 Picardy Place EH1 3JT ☎ 0131 557 6910 🚍 10, 11, 12, 16, 26, 44 or tram to York Place

ANGELS SHARE HOTEL

angelssharehotel.com
This trendy hotel in Edinburgh's West End has comfortable rooms each themed with a Scottish celebrity, from

ACCOMMODATIONS

Apart from the larger, more obvious hotels, Edinburgh has numerous guesthouses and small family-run hotels. The latter will have more rooms, normally all with en-suite facilities; they will probably be licensed to serve alcohol and they will provide breakfast, dinner and sometimes lunch. For something more homelike, bed-and-breakfasts are usually very comfortable, and give you the opportunity to sample a real Scottish breakfast. If you intend to stay outside the city and just go in for individual days to sight-see, it can be worth considering self-catering accommodation (▷ 111, panel). There are several holiday parks nearby that offer holiday homes and touring caravan and camping pitches for the lower budget.

Sean Connery to Sir Chris Hoy. Close to some of Edinburgh's best shopping and nightlife, it also has its own restaurant and late-night cocktail bar.
➕ B6 ✉ 9–11 Hope Street EH2 4EL ☎ 0131 247 7000 🚍 36

THE BALLANTRAE

ballantraehotel.co.uk
This hotel, in a listed Georgian town house in New Town, has 19 spacious rooms with period detail. The honeymoon suite has a four-poster bed and the family room has a Jacuzzi. Next door, the Ballantrae Apartments offer self-catering apartments.
➕ E4 ✉ 8 York Place EH1 3EP ☎ 0131 478 4748 🚍 4, 8, 10, 11, 12, 15, 16, 17, 26, 44, 45 or tram to York Place

CHANNINGS

channings.co.uk
Elegant town house, once the home of Antarctic explorer Sir Ernest Shackleton, offering country-style tranquility in a West End setting. The 41 rooms vary in size but all are decorated with style.
➕ Off map ✉ South Learmonth Gardens EH4 1EZ ☎ 0131 560 2066 🚍 19, 37, 37A

DUNSTANE HOUSE

dunstane-hotel-edinburgh.co.uk
In the city's West End close to Haymarket station, this 1850s Victorian mansion house has retained much of its architectural grandeur, giving a country-house atmosphere. Some of the 16 bedrooms have four-poster beds.
➕ Off map ✉ 4 West Coates, Haymarket EH12 5JQ ☎ 0131 337 6169 🚍 12, 26, 31

EDINBURGH CITY HOTEL

edinburghcityhotel.com
On a site that was once a maternity hospital, this tasteful conversion is close

to central Edinburgh. The 52 spacious bedrooms are smartly modern and well equipped, with fridges. There is a cozy yet stylish bar and restaurant.

🏠 D7 ✉ 79 Lauriston Place EH3 9HZ ☎ 0131 622 7979 🚌 2

HOLYROOD HOTEL

macdonaldhotels.co.uk

This large and impressive business hotel, just a couple of minutes' walk from the Royal Mile and the new Scottish Parliament Building, offers extensive facilities, including conference suites and a spa.

🏠 G6 ✉ Holyrood Road EH8 6AE ☎ 0344 879 9028 🚌 35

HOTEL DU VIN

hotelduvin.com

This classy hotel is at the top end of this price bracket but it's worth looking for one of the good deals available. This former poorhouse and asylum makes much of exposed brickwork and original features. The 47 rooms and suites offer a high level of comfort and decoration. First-class food is served in the hallmark Du Vin bistro, which has a whisky snug for relaxation.

🏠 E7 ✉ Bristo Place, 2 Forrest Road EH1 1EY ☎ 0131 285 1479 🚌 2, 41, 42, 67

THE INN ON THE MILE

theinnonthemile.co.uk

The cozy Inn on the Mile is a bar-restaurant with stylish rooms and a grandstand view of the Royal Mile. Waverley Station is less than a 5-minute walk. There's live music every night except Sunday in the popular bar. Rooms are chic, with perks like free mineral water, fluffy bathrobes and mini-bars. Guests may use the pool at the next-door Radisson Blu for a fee.

SELF-CATERING

If you are planning to stay outside Edinburgh and travel into the city daily, it is worth considering renting self-catering accommodation. The choice is good—you could stay in anything from an idyllic cottage to the wing of a castle. Even in Edinburgh itself, there are self-catering options available. The Edinburgh and Lothian Tourist Board publishes full details of self-catering options in its annual accommodation guide and also provides a reservation service.

🏠 F6 ✉ 82 High Street EH1 1LL ☎ 0131 556 9940 🚌 2, 3, 5, 6, 7, 8, 14, 29, 30, 31, 33, 37

KEW HOUSE

kewhouse.com

Forming part of a listed Victorian terrace, Kew House is spotless throughout and has six bright bedrooms and a comfortable lounge offering supper and snack options. It's located near Murrayfield Stadium and is just a 15-minute walk from the center of Edinburgh.

🏠 Off map ✉ 1 Kew Terrace, Murrayfield EH12 5JE ☎ 0131 313 0700 🚌 12, 26, 31

THE RAEBURN

theraeburn.com

This 10-bedroom boutique hotel in a Georgian town house is within easy reach of city-center sights but is located away from the crowds in bohemian Stockbridge. Rooms are stylish, with roll-top baths and walk-in rain showers. The gastropub-style restaurant serves hearty dishes such as shin of beef and onion pie. For smokers, there's a covered outdoor terrace.

🏠 Off map ✉ 112 Raeburn Place EH4 1HG ☎ 0131 332 7000 🚌 24, 29, 42

Luxury Hotels

BALMORAL

roccofortehotels.com

The Balmoral is an impressive landmark in the heart of the city, its grand clock tower a familiar feature of the city skyline. The 188 bedrooms have a contemporary feel, while retaining the Balmoral's grandeur. The Number One restaurant has a Michelin star and serves exceptional Scottish cuisine.

➕ E5 ✉ 1 Princes Street EH2 2EQ ☎ 0131 556 2414 🚌 3, 10, 17, 23, 24, 27, 44

THE BONHAM

thetownhousecompany.com

This West End hotel offers modern public rooms with mood lighting and striking art, and 48 bedrooms combining high standards of style with 21st-century technology. There is a refreshing contemporary feel throughout. Imaginative, European-influenced dinners in the Restaurant at the Bonham highlight the chef's good use of local fresh produce.

➕ A6 ✉ 35 Drumsheugh Gardens EH3 7RN ☎ 0131 226 6050 🚌 13

GLASSHOUSE

theglasshousehotel.co.uk

Modern glass architecture strikingly embraces the facade of former Lady Glenorchy Church as you enter this chic boutique hotel. The 65 rooms have floor-to-ceiling windows that ensure spectacular views over Calton Hill. There's also a rooftop bar and garden.

➕ F4 ✉ 2 Greenside Place EH1 3AA ☎ 0131 525 8200 🚌 4, 7, 10, 11, 12, 16, 22, 34

THE HOWARD

thehoward.com

Three Georgian houses make up this sophisticated hotel a short walk from Princes Street. The 18 good-size rooms have bathrooms with claw-foot baths, and the elegant day rooms are decked out with chandeliers, sumptuous fabrics and murals.

➕ C3 ✉ 34 Great King Street EH3 6QH ☎ 0131 557 3500 🚌 13

MALMAISON

malmaison.com

This stylish Leith hotel has 100 bedrooms, some decorated in bold stripes, others in subtle tones. Some have views of the port at Leith.

➕ Off map ✉ 1 Tower Place, Leith EH6 7BZ ☎ 0131 468 5000 🚌 16, 22, 35, 36

THE PRINCIPAL EDINBURGH

phcompany.com

After a multimillion-pound refurbishment, the delightful 18th-century George Hotel reopened under a new name in 2016. It boasts 250 rooms and a mini-spa and rooftop lounge with fantastic views toward Edinburgh Castle. The Printing Press serves contemporary Scottish cuisine.

➕ D5 ✉ 19–21 George Street EH2 2PB ☎ 0131 225 1251 🚌 13, 19, 41

THE SCOTSMAN

thescotsmanhotel.co.uk

The former head office of *The Scotsman* newspaper in Old Town is now a luxury hotel, with 69 traditionally decorated rooms. The North Bridge Brasserie offers fine dining and the subterranean Escape leisure club has an unusual stainless steel swimming pool.

➕ E5 ✉ 20 North Bridge EH1 1YT ☎ 0131 556 5565 🚌 3, 5, 7, 30, 31, 33, 37

Need to Know

Use this section to help you plan your visit to Edinburgh. We have suggested the best ways to get around the city, and have included other useful information for when you are there.

Planning Ahead

When to Go

Edinburgh lies on the eastern side of Scotland, which is cooler, windier and drier than the west. At any time of year you are likely to meet rain, but the chances are it will not last for long. Some tourist sights close in winter, but major city museums stay open year-round.

TIME

GMT (Greenwich Mean Time) is standard. BST (British Summer Time) is 1 hour ahead (late Mar–late Oct).

AVERAGE DAILY MAXIMUM TEMPERATURES

JAN	FEB	MAR	APR	MAY	JUN	JUL	AUG	SEP	OCT	NOV	DEC
39°F	39°F	43°F	48°F	54°F	61°F	63°F	61°F	59°F	54°F	45°F	41°F
4°C	4°C	6°C	9°C	12°C	16°C	17°C	16°C	15°C	12°C	7°C	5°C

Spring (March to May) has the best chance of clear skies and sunny days.

Summer (June to August) is unpredictable—it may be hot and sunny, but it can also be cloudy and wet. This is the time you can get *haar* (sea mist) that shrouds the city in thick mist, although this can happen at other times of the year as well.

Autumn (September to November) is usually more settled and there's a good chance of fine weather, but nothing is guaranteed.

Winter (December to February) can be cold, dark, wet and dreary, but there are also sparkling clear, sunny days of frost, when the light is brilliant.

WHAT'S ON

January *Burns Night* (25 Jan): the birthday of Scotland's bard, celebrated throughout Scotland with haggis and whisky.

March/April *Edinburgh Science Festival:* science and technology events at various venues.

Ceilidh Culture: events centered around traditional Scottish arts.

May *Bank of Scotland Imaginate Festival:* Britain's largest performing arts festival for young people.

June *Edinburgh International Film Festival:* (▷ 41, panel).

Royal Highland Show: Scotland's biggest agricultural show.

Edinburgh Marathon.

July/August *Edinburgh Jazz & Blues Festival:* 10 days of jazz performed by big names and new talent.

August *Edinburgh International Festival:* over three weeks, some of the world's best plays, opera, music and dance.

Edinburgh Festival Fringe: A chance for the amateurs to join the professionals.

Edinburgh Military Tattoo: (▷ 5).

International Book Festival: occupies a tented village in Charlotte Square.

Mela: a vibrant celebration of cultural diversity with music, dance and street performers.

October *Scottish International Storytelling Festival:* attracts storytellers from home and abroad.

November/December *Edinburgh's Christmas:* German and Scottish Christmas markets, ice rink, Ferris wheel and more.

December/January *Edinburgh Hogmanay:* (▷ 13).

Edinburgh Online

visitscotland.com
The official VisitScotland website, with a comprehensive database of information covering everything from weather, transport and events to shopping, nightlife and accommodations throughout Scotland.

eif.co.uk
A comprehensive guide to What's On at the Edinburgh International Festival.

edinburghguide.com
An informative guide to attractions, entertainment, recreation, eating out and accommodations, plus links to other sites.

nms.ac.uk
The National Museum of Scotland looks after many of Scotland's important museum collections. Its website provides detailed information about the museums in its care.

undiscoveredscotland.co.uk
An online guide to Scotland. The Edinburgh section has many useful links to other good sources of information.

nts.org.uk
The National Trust for Scotland looks after historic buildings in Scotland, including some in Edinburgh. Its website gives updated information about all the properties it is responsible for.

historicenvironment.scot
This website has information on more than 300 listed buildings and ancient sites safeguarded by Historic Scotland.

thehotelguru.com
More than 30 of Edinburgh's best boutique hotels and guesthouses are reviewed and can be booked on this website, which also lists places to stay throughout Scotland and the rest of the UK.

TRAVEL SITES

fodors.com
A complete travel-planning site. You can research prices and weather; reserve air tickets, cars and rooms; pose questions to (and get answers from) fellow visitors; and find links to other sites.

theAA.com
The AA's site helps you to find accommodations in the city, as well as pubs and restaurants.

ONLINE ACCESS

Free WiFi access is available at many cafés and bars throughout the city center (including branches of Caffè Nero and Costa Coffee) and in almost all hotels and guesthouses. Surprisingly, some larger hotels belonging to international chains still charge extra for WiFi in bedrooms—a service that most smaller places provide free.

Getting There

ENTRY REQUIREMENTS

● Visitors from outside the UK must have a passport, valid for at least six months from the date of entry.
● Before traveling, visitors from outside the UK should check visa requirements. See ukvisas.gov.uk or usembassy.org.uk/scotland.
● Photographic ID is required for all flights. Only passports are accepted.

CUSTOMS

● EU nationals do not have to declare goods imported for their own use, although you may be questioned by customs officials if you have large amounts of certain items.
● The limits for non-EU visitors are 200 cigarettes or 50 cigars or 250g of tobacco; 1 liter of alcohol (over 22 percent alcohol) or 2 liters of wine; 50g of perfume.

AIRPORTS

There are direct flights to Edinburgh from other parts of the UK and from continental Europe. United flies direct from Chicago and Air Canada flies direct from Toronto. Several airlines fly direct from North America to Glasgow International Airport (glasgowairport.com), which is around 90 minutes from Edinburgh by road or train.

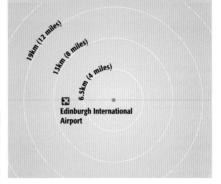

19km (12 miles)
13km (8 miles)
6.5km (4 miles)

⊠ **Edinburgh International Airport**

FROM EDINBURGH INTERNATIONAL AIRPORT

Edinburgh International Airport (edinburghairport.com) is 20–30 minutes from the city center by bus, tram or cab.

The tram runs between the airport and York Place, with intermediate stops at Murrayfield, Haymarket Station and along Princes Street. Airlink 100 buses operate between the airport and Waverley Bridge, in the city center, every 10 minutes and cost £4.50 one way or £7.50 round trip. Service 35 buses leave from stand 21, outside the Arrivals Hall, for Ocean Terminal in Leith. Stops include the Scottish Parliament and the Palace of Holyroodhouse: flat fare is £1.60. The N22 night bus also leaves from the stand outside the Arrivals Hall and runs from the airport to the city center and Ocean Terminal in Leith. Journey time is around 45 minutes: flat fare is £3.

The airport cab rank is opposite the Arrivals Hall, on the ground floor of the parking garage. The cab fare to the city center is £20–£30.

INTERNAL FLIGHTS

Within the UK and Ireland, you can fly to Edinburgh from Belfast, Birmingham, Cardiff, Cork, Derry, Dublin, East Midlands, Exeter, Kirkwall, Knock, London (City, Gatwick, Heathrow, Luton and Stansted), Manchester, Newquay, Norwich, Shannon, Southampton, Stornoway and Sumburgh.

ARRIVING BY RAIL

Edinburgh has two major rail stations: Edinburgh Haymarket and Edinburgh Waverley. Waverley is a main hub for travel within Scotland, and has tourist information desks and other facilities. Regular trains connect Edinburgh with England, via the West Coast Main Line or East Coast Main Line. Most internal services are run by First ScotRail (firstgroup.com/scotland). For further details of fares and services contact the National Rail Enquiry Service (tel 0191 387 1387, nationalrail.co.uk).

ARRIVING BY COACH

Coaches arrive in Edinburgh from England, Wales and all over Scotland at the St. Andrew Street bus station. The main coach companies operating to and from here are National Express (nationalexpress.com) and Scottish Citylink (citylink.co.uk). There is a taxi rank on North St. David Street which can be accessed directly from the arrivals concourse.

ARRIVING BY CAR

One-way systems, narrow streets, red routes and dedicated bus routes and a 20mph (32km/h) speed limit make driving in the historic city center difficult. Limited on-street parking is mostly pay-and-display between 8.30am–6.30pm Mon–Sat. There are some-designated parking areas, to the south of Princes Street; the biggest is at Greenside Place, off Leith Street. Petrol stations are normally open Mon–Sat 6am–10pm, Sun 8am–8pm, though some (often self-service) are open 24 hours. All take credit cards.

INSURANCE

Check your insurance coverage and buy a supplementary policy if needed. EU nationals receive reduced-cost medical treatment with an EHIC card. Obtain this card before leaving home. Full health and travel insurance is still advised.

CONSULATES

All embassies are located in London but the following consulates are based in Edinburgh:
- French Consulate ✉ 11 Randolph Crescent EH3 7TT ☎ 0131 225 7954
- German Consulate ✉ 16 Eglinton Crescent EH12 5DG ☎ 0131 337 2323
- Irish Consulate ✉ 16 Randolph Crescent EH3 7TT ☎ 0131 226 7711
- Netherlands Consulate ✉ 38 Melville Street EH3 7HA ☎ 0131 510 0323
- Spanish Consulate ✉ 63 North Castle Street EH2 3LJ ☎ 0131 220 1843
- US Consulate ✉ 3 Regent Terrace EH7 5BW ☎ 0131 556 8315

Getting Around

● The official source of information for tourists is VisitScotland, which has a very useful website, visitscotland.com.

● Edinburgh and Scotland Information Centre
✉ 3 Princes Street EH2 2QP ☎ 0131 473 3868
🕐 May–Jun, Sep, Mon–Sat 9–7, Sun 10–7; Jul–Aug Mon–Sat 9–8, Sun 10–8; Apr, Oct Mon–Sat 9–6, Sun 10–6; Nov–Mar Mon–Sat 9–5, Sun 10–5.

● Edinburgh Airport Tourist Information Desk
✉ East terminal EH12 9DN
☎ 0131 473 3690
🕐 Apr–Oct daily 6.30am–10.30pm; Nov–Mar daily 7am–9pm.

LOST PROPERTY

● Property found and handed to the police is sent to Police Headquarters:
✉ Fettes Avenue ☎ 0131 311 3131 🕐 Mon–Fri 9–5.

● There are lost property departments at Edinburgh Airport ☎ 0131 344 3486; Waverley train station ☎ 0131 550 2333; and Lothian buses ✉ Annandale Street, off Leith Walk ☎ 0131 558 8858 🕐 Mon–Fri 10–1.30.

● Report losses of passports to the police.

BY BUS AND TRAM

Edinburgh's city bus network (lothianbuses.com) reaches every part of the city and beyond. Services include a 24-hour Airlink 100 service (edinburghairport.com/transport-links/buses-and-coaches) between Edinburgh International Airport and Waverley Bridge in the city center, with intermediate stops including Haymarket Station. A flat-fare, one-way bus or tram ride costs £1.60 for an adult (exact fare only) and 80p for children (5–11 years). Under-fives travel free. Day tickets permitting 24 hours unlimited bus and tram travel (within the central zone) cost £4 for an adult, £2 for a child and £8.50 for a family of four, and can be bought online from lothianbuses.com or from the city-center Travelshop at Waverley Bridge. You can also buy a Citysmart card, which stores 10–50 single-trip tickets, or download M-tickets to your mobile device (minimum spend £10).

TICKETS

Find timetables and fare information online at lothianbuses.com or at Travelshops at Waverley Bridge, 27 Hanover Street, Haymarket Station or Edinburgh Airport (Mon–Thu 9–7, Tue–Wed, Fri 9–6, Sat 9–5.30, Sun 10–5.30).

TAXIS

Licensed taxis operate a reliable day and night service. Fares are metered and strictly regulated. Cabs can be hailed on the street or found at designated ranks at the airport, Haymarket Station, Waverley Bridge (outside Waverley Station), outside St. Andrew Square coach terminus on North St. Andrew Street and outside Balmoral Hotel at the east end of Princes Street. Private hire cabs can also be booked in advance or called by phone (City Cabs 0131 228 1211; Central Radio taxis 0131 229 2468).

CAR RENTAL

The major international car rental brands have desks at the airport, just outside the main Arrivals Hall. Several have city-center outlets.

Some (including Hertz and Enterprise) advertise these as being located at Waverley Station but they may be a short walk away, on or near Picardy Place at the top of Leith Walk. If you plan on renting a car, choose accommodations that offers private car parking—it's almost impossible to find free parking space in most of the city.

BICYCLE RENTAL
Edinburgh's largest bike rental outfit is Biketrax (tel 0131 228 6633, biketrax.co.uk), which has 21-speed hybrid city bikes, 16-speed light-weights and folding bikes. Cycle Scotland (tel 0131 556 5560, cyclescotland.co.uk) rents mountain and road bikes, hybrids and tandems.

ORGANIZED SIGHTSEEING
A guided tour is a good way to gain more in-depth knowledge about Edinburgh. If time is short, take one of the open-top buses that wind their way around the city sights; all tours depart from Waverley Bridge and there are four types to choose from, including one where you can hop on and hop off at your leisure (tel 0131 554 4494, edinburghtour.com). A commentary is available in a number of languages.

Various companies offer coach tours in and around the city. Try Rabbie's Trail Burners (tel 0131 226 3133, rabbies.com), who run mini-coach (16-seater) tours to destinations such as Loch Ness and St. Andrews.

For those who prefer two wheels, another option is Edinburgh Bike Tours (tel 07753 136676, edinburghbiketours.co.uk), which offers full-day and half-day guided tours with all equipment provided.

Mercat Walking Tours offers walks where you explore secret underground vaults, ghost walks and fascinating history tours with dramatic commentaries (Mercat House, 28 Blair Street EH1 1QR, tel 0131 225 5445, mercattours.com). Sandemans run free, three-hour walking tours year round. Tours usually leave at 10, 11, 2 and 6.30 from Starbucks Café by Tron Kirk on High Street (neweuropetours.eu).

VISITORS WITH DISABILITIES
● Capability Scotland (✉ 11 Ellersly Road, Edinburgh EH12 6HY ☎ 0131 337 9876; capability-scotland.org.uk) can advise on travel requirements to ensure a smooth trip.

● disabledgo.com is an internet service giving access information to people with disabilities, as well as other advice useful when visiting Edinburgh. Restaurants, cafés, shops and attractions are all covered.

● A wide range of information for visitors with disabilities can be found in VisitScotland's publication *Practical Information for Visitors with Disabilities*, available from the tourist board or from tourist offices.

STUDENT VISITORS
● Students can get reduced-cost entry to some museums and attractions by showing a valid student card.
● Budget accommodations are available (▷ 109).
● There are reduced fares on buses and trains for under 16s.

Essential Facts

CREDIT/DEBIT CARDS

● Credit and debit cards are widely accepted.
● ATMs are readily available anywhere in the city.

MONEY

Scotland's currency is pounds sterling (£), in notes of £5, £10, £20, £50 and £100. Coins are issued in values of 1p, 2p, 5p, 10p, 20p, 50p, £1 and £2. England's notes are legal tender in Scotland. Three Scottish banks (Bank of Scotland, Royal Bank of Scotland and Clydesdale Bank) also issue their own sterling notes, which circulate throughout Scotland. These may not be accepted elsewhere in the UK and are hard to exchange outside the UK, so spend them (or exchange them for Bank of England notes at a bank) before leaving Scotland.

TIPPING

In upscale restaurants, a tip of 10 percent is the norm. In smaller eating places, a tip is welcomed but not mandatory. Taxi drivers, tour guides, hairdressers and bar staff (except in more expensive establishments) do not normally expect to be tipped, though a gratuity for better-than-average service will be welcome.

ELECTRICITY

● Britain is on 240 volts AC, and plugs have three square pins. If you are bringing an electrical appliance from another country where the voltage is the same, a plug adaptor will suffice. If the voltage is different, as in the US—110 volts—you need a converter.
● Small appliances such as razors can run on a 50-watt converter, while heating appliances, irons and hairdryers require a 1,600-watt converter.

EMERGENCY TELEPHONE NUMBERS

● For Police, Ambulance, Fire call 999 or 112.
● For non-emergency police enquiries call 101.
● If you break down driving your own car you can call the Automobile Association and join on the spot if you are not already a member (tel 0800 0852721). Check if your home country membership entitles you to reciprocal assistance. If you are driving a rental car, call the emergency number in your documentation.

MEDICINES AND MEDICAL TREATMENT

● Citizens from the EU are entitled to free or reduced-cost NHS (National Health Service) treatment—bring the EHIC card from your home country. Full health and travel insurance is still advised.
● Those visiting from outside the EU should have full travel and health insurance.
● For medical emergencies call 999 or 112 or go to the nearest hospital accident and emergency department.
● The 24-hour A&E department is at the Royal Infirmary of Edinburgh (51 Little France Crescent, Old Dalkeith Road EH16 4SA, tel 0131 536 1000).
● For minor injuries, the Western General Hospital (Crewe Road South EH4 2XU, tel 0131 537 1000, open daily 9–9) has a walk-in service. For advice from specialist nurse practitioners call NHS24 on 111 or see nhs24.com.
● To find the nearest dentist, call Lothian Dental Advice Line (tel 0131 536 4800). Walk-in

dental treatment is available at Chalmers Dental Centre (3 Chalmers Street, tel 0131 536 4800, open Mon–Thu 9–4.45, Fri 9–4.15).

● Pharmacies and large supermarkets sell a range of medicines over the counter but items such as antibiotics require a prescription.

● There are no 24-hour pharmacies in Edinburgh. Boots the Chemist (48 Shandwick Place, tel 0131 225 6757) has the longest opening hours (Mon–Fri 8am–9pm, Sat 8–6, Sun 10.30–4.30).

● If you are planning to spend much time in the countryside around Edinburgh in high summer, beware of "midgies," the Scottish relative of tiny biters known in the US as "no-see'ums." Most pharmacies sell a range of remedies that will help prevent them from blighting a picnic.

● Bear in mind, too, that in high summer the Scottish sun can burn, despite cool breezes. Use sunblock and sunscreen, particularly on young children.

NATIONAL HOLIDAYS
● New Year's Day (1 January)
● New Year's Holiday (2 January)
● Good Friday
● Easter Monday
● First Monday in May
● Last Monday in May
● First Monday in August
● Last Monday in August
● Christmas Day (25 December)
● Boxing Day (26 December)
● Most places of interest close on New Year's Day, 1 May and Christmas, while others close on all public holidays.

OPENING TIMES
● Banks: Mon–Fri 9.30–4.30; larger branches open Sat morning.
● Post offices: Mon–Fri 9–5.30, Sat 9–12.
● Shops: most shops open daily 9–5, including Sundays.
● Museums: opening times vary widely, see individual entries.

PERSONAL SAFETY
● Levels of violent crime are relatively low but there are areas to avoid, as in every city. At night these include the backstreet and dockside areas of Leith, *wynds* (narrow lanes) off the Royal Mile, the footpaths across the Meadows and unlit urban areas.

● Scottish police officers wear a peaked flat hat with a black-and-white check band and are friendly and approachable.

● Petty theft is the most common problem, so don't carry more cash than you need and beware of pickpockets, especially in the main tourist areas and on public transport. Take care of bags and do not leave them on backs of chairs.

TOILETS
Public toilets are hard to find in the city center. There is a small charge to use toilets at rail and bus stations. Pubs and café-bars frown on visitors who use their toilets without buying a drink. Smaller cafés which do not serve alcohol are not required to have toilet facilities. There are free toilets in all the museums and art galleries and in the Central Library and the National Library of Scotland, both on George IV Bridge.

NEWSPAPERS AND MAGAZINES

● Subscribe free to *The Edinburgh Reporter* (theedinburghreporter. com) for twice-daily online reports of events, sports fixtures, new restaurant and bar openings and more.

● *The Leither* (free in the best bars from Leith to Broughton and Stockbridge) speaks its own distinctive voice about local events and global issues.

● *The Skinny* (theskinny. co.uk) offers "independent cultural journalism" to a mainly student audience looking for great nights out.

● *The One O'Clock Gun* is an oddball literary broadsheet, distributed free in selected Old Town and New Town bars.

TELEPHONE SERVICES

● Various companies offer Directory Enquiries services. The British Telecom numbers are:

● Directory Enquiries
☎ 118 500

● International Directory Enquiries ☎ 118 505

● International Operator
☎ 155

● Operator ☎ 100

POST OFFICES

● The main post office is at St. James Centre, St. Andrew Square. It's open Mon–Sat 9–5.30. Most other post offices are open on weekdays and Saturday mornings.

● Many newspaper shops and supermarkets sell stamps.

● Postboxes are painted red; collection times are shown on each box.

RADIO AND TELEVISION

● Scotland is served by UK national radio stations, and most Scottish regions and cities also have their own stations. Edinburgh's Radio Forth (97.3FM) broadcasts a mix of news, music, traffic reports and weather forecasts.

● BBC Radio Scotland (94.3FM) broadcasts a similar mix but covers the whole of Scotland.

● Digital and satellite TV stations available in Scotland include all BBC national channels, ITV, STV, CNN and Sky channels.

TELEPHONES AND WIFI

● The code for Edinburgh is 0131. Omit the area code when making a local call.

● Payphones can be found at the airport, coach station, railway stations and elsewhere in the city center. They accept 10p, 20p, 50p and £1. Credit and debit cards can also be used. BT (British Telecom) payphones cost a minimum of 60p for cash payments and £1.20 when paying by card; the minimum charge includes a 40p connection charge and two calling time units of 10p.

● Mobile phone coverage is good but not all US and Canadian cell phones will work in the UK, and roaming charges may be very high.

● To call the US from Scotland dial 00 1, followed by the number. To call Scotland from the US, dial 011 44, then omit the 0 from the area code

● Free wireless internet is provided throughout the city center by City of Edinburgh's EdiFree WiFi system. Find a map of WiFi hotspots at edinburghfreewifi.com.

Language

Standard English is the official language of Scotland, and is spoken everywhere. However, as with other parts of Britain, the Scottish people have their own variations on the language and the way it is spoken. You should have no difficulty understanding the people of Edinburgh, who tend automatically to moderate their accent when speaking to non-Scots. But many Scottish words and phrases are used in everyday conversation.

COMMON WORDS AND PHRASES	
auld	old
awfy	very
aye/naw	yes/no
belong	come from
ben	hill, mountain
bide	live
birle	spin, turn
blether	to chatter, gossip
bonnie	pretty, attractive
braw	fine, good
burn	stream
canny	cunning, clever
ceilidh	party or dance
couthy	comfortable
douce	gentle and kind
dram	a measure of whisky
een	eyes
fash	bother
gae	go
gloaming	dusk
guttered	drunk
haar	sea mist
Hogmanay	New Year's Eve
ken	to know
kirk	church
lassie	girl
lum	chimney
messages	shopping
nicht	night
och	oh
Sassenach	non-Scottish person
trews	tartan trousers
wee	small

Timeline

EARLY SETTLERS

The area was first settled by hunting tribes around 3000BC and in about 1000BC the first farmers were joined by immigrant Beaker People, who introduced pottery and metalworking skills. Parts of Scotland were held by the Romans for a short time. After their departure in the 5th century AD the area suffered waves of invasion.

THE MACALPINS

Northumbrians held southern Scotland for 33 years, but were defeated in 1018 by MacAlpin king Malcolm II. Malcolm III married Margaret, sister of Edgar Atheling, heir to the English throne, but was usurped by William the Conqueror.

From left to right: Robert the Bruce statue; James VI of Scotland; the Forth Rail Bridge; posters for the Edinburgh Festival; Holyrood Park hosts Fringe Festival events

6th century *AD* The Gododdin, a Celtic tribe, make their seat at Dun Eidinn.

638 Dun Eidinn falls to the Angles of Northumbria and is renamed Edinburgh.

1018 Edinburgh and Lothian conquered by Malcolm II.

1110 David I builds St. Margaret's Chapel.

1128 Foundation of Holyrood Abbey.

1296–1357 Scottish Wars of Independence. Castle alternates between English and Scottish control but Scotland retains independence.

1437 Edinburgh becomes royal capital.

1501 James I begins Palace of Holyroodhouse.

1544 English forces sack Edinburgh but fail to take Castle.

1603 James VI succeeds to English throne as James I, thus uniting the Scottish and English crowns, and moves court to London.

1707 Scottish Parliament ratifies the Act of Union and Edinburgh ceases to be Scotland's seat of government.

1767 Construction of New Town begins.

1776 North Bridge completed. Royal Observatory opens on Calton Hill.

1822 George IV is the first British monarch to visit Edinburgh since Charles II in 1651.

1847 North British Railway advertises first Edinbugh–London service.

1890 Forth Bridge carries first trains between Edinburgh and northern Scotland.

1947 First Edinburgh International Festival held.

1964 Forth Road Bridge opened.

1997 Most Scots vote for devolution, allowing for a Scottish Parliament within the UK.

1999 The Scottish Parliament sits for the first time since 1707.

2004 Scottish Parliament moves into new building at Holyrood.

2014 Referendum on Scottish independence results in a "no" vote.

2015 Forth (Rail) Bridge granted Unesco World Heritage status.

2017 Opening of Queensferry Crossing, a major new road bridge next to historic Forth Bridges.

EDINBURGH'S FAMOUS

Some of Edinburgh's most famous citizens have had a significant impact on our lives. Alexander Graham Bell invented the telephone in 1847, and anaesthetics were pioneered by James Young Simpson. John Knox reformed Scotland's religion and architect Robert Adam and artists Henry Raeburn and Allan Ramsay brought their flair to the buildings of the city. The literary impact has been phenomenal, through the romances of Sir Walter Scott, who was born in the city in 1771, and the detective stories of Sir Arthur Conan Doyle. More fame comes from Robert Louis Stevenson, author of *Kidnapped* and *Treasure Island*, who was born here in 1850, and actor Sean Connery, who spent his early days here.

Index

Edinburgh 25 Best

WRITTEN BY Hilary Weston and Jackie Staddon
ADDITIONAL WRITING BY Sally Roy
UPDATED BY Robin Gauldie
SERIES EDITOR Clare Ashton
COVER DESIGN Chie Ushio, Yuko Inagaki
DESIGN WORK Liz Baldin
IMAGE RETOUCHING AND REPRO Ian Little

Published in the United Kingdom by AA Publishing

ISBN 978-0-1475-4706-4

FOURTH EDITION

SPECIAL SALES
This book is available for special discounts for bulk purchases for sales promotions or premiums. For more information, email specialmarkets@penguinrandomhouse.com.

Color separation by AA Digital Department
Printed and bound by Leo Paper Products, China

10 9 8 7 6 5 4 3 2 1